Barcode in Back

Glory Days

A Play and History of the '46 Stelco Strike

Glory Days

A Play and History of the ’46 Stelco Strike

Bill Freeman

Playwrights Canada Press
Toronto • Canada

Playwrights Canada Press
The Canadian Drama Publisher
215 Spadina Avenue, Suite 230, Toronto, Ontario CANADA M5T 2C7
416-703-0013 fax 416-408-3402
orders@playwrightscanada.com • www.playwrightscanada.com

Financial support provided by the taxpayers of Canada and Ontario through the Canada Council for the Arts and the Department of Canadian Heritage through the Book Publishing Industry Development Programme, and the Ontario Arts Council.

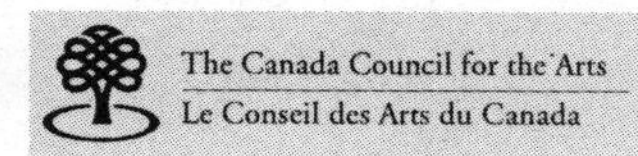

Front cover photo of the 2006 production by Roy Timm. *l to r:* Paolo Mancini, Caden Douglas, Ryan Hollyman, George Masswohl, Tara Hughes, Stephanie McNamara, Lina Giornofelice, Tim Campbell.
Production Editor/Cover design: JLArt

Library and Archives Canada Cataloguing in Publication

Freeman, Bill, 1938-
Glory days : a play and history of the '46 Stelco strike / Bill Freeman.

ISBN 978-0-88754-668-6

1. Steel Company of Canada Strike, Hamilton, Ont., 1946--Drama.
2. United Steelworkers of America. Local 1005 (Hamilton, Ont.)--Drama.
3. Steel Company of Canada Strike, Hamilton, Ont., 1946--History.
4. United Steelworkers of America. Local 1005 (Hamilton, Ont.)--History.
I. Title.

PS8561.R378G58 2007 C812'.54 C2007-901617-0

First edition: April 2007.
Printed and bound by AGMV Marquis at Quebec, Canada.

for trade unionists everywhere

Contents

Acknowledgements and Author's Notes

In Hamilton the 1946 Stelco strike still looms large in the collective memory of the people of the city. For many it has almost mythical proportions of a time when steelworkers challenged one of the largest and most powerful companies in the country, led by Hugh Hilton, a virulently anti-union company president, and decisively won a victory for union recognition on the picket line.

When I lived in Hamilton in the 1960s and 70s, I met many people whose lives were shaped by that event. The veterans of the '46 strike played leadership roles in the union movement, on city council, and many of the political organizations and social clubs of the city. Often I attended events and listened to stories about the strike. Those stories were the genesis of *Glory Days.* So the first thanks I would like to offer is to the people in the city of Hamilton who lived through those traumatic days.

In the spring and summer of 1976 I interviewed a large number of members of Local 1005 of the Steelworkers. That work was ultimately published as a book, *1005: Political Life in a Local Union.* Even then many of the members active in the union local were strike veterans. I recorded and transcribed all of those interviews. As I worked on them I came to realize that the interviews were a treasure of information about working class life in Hamilton in the 1930s and '40s, working conditions in the steel mills and the struggle to establish unions. Many of the stories and incidents that appear in the play come directly out of those interviews.

I thought about writing another book about Hamilton featuring this period but the drama of the strike had captured my imagination. I wanted to do a work that had popular appeal and could reach a large number of people. A play seemed to be just the right vehicle. Some time in the mid 1980s I approached Peter Mandia, the founder and artistic director of Theatre Aquarius, Hamilton's professional theatre company, to see if he might be interested in a play based on the '46 strike. Peter was enthusiastic and that enthusiasm and the commitment of the theatre pushed the project to the next level.

I have a great love of the magic of live performance, and I had written a play for young people before I started work on *Glory Days*, but most of my writing career up until then had been devoted to writing books.

I needed help to take the events of the '46 strike and shape them into dramatic theatre. Peter Mandia and the cast of the first production in 1988 helped me do that. It was a bruising experience to sit through workshops and rehearsals listening to the criticisms of the script by professional actors and the director but I am thankful for those efforts. It improved the script immeasurably. That original production of *Glory Days* was an artistic and critical success that I cherish. I know I could not have achieved it alone.

The careers of writers are driven by their projects, and after *Glory Days* I moved on to other books and film scripts. Then, one day in 2004, Max Reimer, who had become the artistic director of Theatre Aquarius after Peter's untimely death, called me to say that the theatre would like to remount *Glory Days.* Would I like to be involved? Would I!? I was overjoyed to be given the opportunity to give *Glory Days* new life.

Working on the remount of the play was a very positive experience. Max and I agreed that the play needed revisions and Lee MacDougall, a playwright and actor, was brought in to work with me on the script. Lee's vast theatrical experience helped to sharpen scenes and made the play flow from action to action in a seamless way. Lee went on to direct the production. His vision is now part of the fabric of *Glory Days.*

I am often asked, what is the difference between the two versions of the play? In essence there is little difference. *Glory Days* is about a group of people who live though the momentous events of the '46 strike. The characters and the conflict are the same in both versions. The most striking difference is that in the initial performance the actors often talked directly to the audience. That helped to move the action forward and tell the audience what had happened to the characters in intervening time. Today that technique is viewed as old fashioned and in the second version of the play that information is given to the audience through the dialogue.

The version of the play in this book follows the 2006 performance with two exceptions. We had hoped to connect the play to modern events by focusing on the threatened bankruptcy of Stelco. The opening and closing scenes imagined a community meeting where different points of view about Stelco and the strike were discussed. By the time the play was presented, the bankruptcy crisis had passed and those two scenes now seem out of place. I have rewritten those scenes and they are now much like the first version of the play.

A performance in theatre is the work of many people. The writer may be the originator but by no means the only creator of the work. *Glory Days* is a play with music; the music grows naturally out of the script. Charles T. Cozens was the composer and musical director of both versions of *Glory Days* and his contribution was an essential part of the play. Charles has written "The Development of Music for the Stage Play *Glory Days*" to describe how he achieved the musical component of the play.

I would like to make special mention of all of the people at Theatre Aquarius who made this production a success, from the set builders to the box office and those who work in the office. Without their teamwork the production would not have happened.

Special thanks go to Jean Paton, who edited this work, and finally a bow to Playwrights Canada Press and its publisher, Angela Rebeiro. Playwrights Canada Press continues to perform a vital role in keeping plays alive in this country.

—BF

Steel, Labour and the '46 Strike

Glory Days opens with these lines.

> **BILLY** Maybe some of you here tonight know something about the Stelco strike of 1946. The "Glory Days" as some have called it. That strike was a victory, a milestone for the people of Hamilton – the people of Canada. It changed things for us all.

In order to understand how a strike can have such an impact on the lives of people we have to leave the theatre and venture into the world of business and unions.

The Founding of Stelco

The Steel Company of Canada, or Stelco as we know it today, emerged in 1910, but the history of steel in this country goes much further back. During the French era, iron was smelted in a small foundry at Saint-Maurice, Quebec. The first industrial production of steel was on Cape Breton Island in Nova Scotia in the 1850s, but it was the National Policy of Prime Minister John A. Macdonald that ensured the success of the steel industry and manufacturing in Canada.[1]

Politics and business have been intertwined in this country since Canada was formed. By the 1860s the United States was a leading industrial power. The railways provided good transportation between the eastern provinces of Canada and the United States, and cheap American products flooded into the country, driving many local firms out of business. A huge controversy ensued. Canadians, particularly those who lived in the cities, argued that Canada needed a system of protective tariffs that taxed goods coming into Canada, giving local manufacturers an advantage. Farmers and people in small towns opposed high tariffs that would put up the price of goods. After considerable debate, the Macdonald government enacted the National Policy of high tariffs in 1879: Canada was on its way to becoming an industrial nation.

Canadian historians still debate the impact of the National Policy, but there is little doubt that it provided a huge incentive to the steel industry. The price of imported American steel products immediately went up and steel companies in this country had the chance to become highly profitable. In the 1890s a group of wealthy New York businessmen decided to take advantage of the high tariffs and began searching for a site to establish a steel mill in Canada. They chose to locate in Hamilton.

There are a number of reasons for their choice. Of prime importance was the Hamilton harbour, one of the best harbours on the Great Lakes. Excellent railway connections linked the city to its markets in Canada and to the large American steel-making centres of the time, like Pittsburgh. Industrial production had become concentrated in Southern Ontario in the last decades of the nineteenth century, partly due to its rapidly growing population. Hamilton had a history of industrial production: many small companies produced iron products such as stoves and farm implements; there was a pool of skilled labour with experience in the metal trades.

There were some disadvantages to Hamilton's location. The major raw materials needed in the steel-making process had to be brought long distances. Coal had to be transported by railroad from the Appalachian coal fields of Pennsylvania, and iron ore shipped from the mines at the head of Lake Superior. In the early days the ore was brought by lake freighters to Point Edward on Lake Huron and then shipped by rail to Hamilton. Later it was brought through the Welland Canal right into Hamilton Harbour. [2] Limestone and scrap, the other two major raw materials, are found locally.

There was one other important factor that led to the choice of Hamilton. City council offered the company a variety of incentives that included tax exemptions and seventy-five acres of free land. The land was a local beauty spot called Huckleberry Point, on the shore of the bay in the east end. The city also offered a $100,000 cash bonus if a blast furnace and open hearth were built on the land. The company accepted the offer in 1893, and soon Huckleberry Point became one of the most important sites of heavy industry in the country.

There were problems. The original group of financers "fell under suspicion for financial malpractice" [3] and were replaced with investors from Hamilton. Various construction and technical problems plagued the project. The most serious was that the stack of the blast furnace blew down in a storm. But finally, in 1896, the company began producing steel.

From its beginning, the Hamilton Steel and Iron Company, as it was then called, was an integrated steel-making facility with blast furnaces and open hearth units. The company developed some finishing mills and shipped product to others around the country. Most Canadian foundries up until this time produced iron products by reheating scrap or pig iron. Stelco continued to make pig iron, but also produced steel, a much harder and more durable product manufactured by combining iron with carbon at high temperatures.

The early years of the company and the steel industry were difficult. Production expanded rapidly in the boom period that preceded the First World War. New investments were made to increase production and output grew dramatically. The primary steel producers in the country were profitable but the finishing mills, located primarily in Montreal, were struggling for survival. Often product flooded the market, driving prices down. There were dramatic swings in prices; financial ruin for the entire industry seemed imminent.

A young financial wizard by the name of Max Aitken solved this problem. In 1910 Aitken organized the merger of Canadian steel companies including Hamilton Steel and Iron as well as a number of finishing mills. The new company was to be called The Steel Company of Canada, soon to be nicknamed Stelco. As part of the agreement, control of the merged company was to remain with the Hamilton group and soon a decision was made to concentrate development at Huckleberry Point in the city's east end.[4]

After the merger, the company was able to get new financing; they built new finishing mills and increased the capacity of the open-hearth mills. By 1913 Stelco had one of the most modern steel mills in the world. With the onset of the First World War in 1914, demand for steel skyrocketed. The company produced shells for the army and steel for every aspect of war production. Domestic demand for steel also grew dramatically. Profits were substantial; the company finally was on a firm financial footing.

The Unions

The trade union movement paralleled the growth of industry in the city. As early as 1833, when Hamilton was little more than a local market town, a branch of the typographical union was established. In the 1870s, when the city was a growing railway and industrial centre, its unions led the nine-hour-a-day movement, which briefly became a major force in Ontario.

Through the last decades of the nineteenth and the early twentieth centuries, Hamilton unions grew in numbers and strength. Even in those early days union members recognized that they had to struggle on two different levels. They had to gain better wages and working conditions from their employers, but they also needed political support to achieve legislation on issues like hours of work, safety and health.

In the industrial cities of Canada there was an increasing polarization between the workers on the one hand and the owners and managers on the other. It was not unusual for the government to intervene on the side of employers. In 1906 the Hamilton Street Railway employees went on strike. The company brought in scabs from Buffalo and tried to keep the streetcars running. This led to a number of disturbances where streetcars were attacked and windows smashed. The city government called in the militia to restore order. The mayor read "The Riot Act." A large crowd of strike supporters gathered on the street, the militia on horseback drew their swords and charged the crowd. Several people were injured, but miraculously no one was killed.[5]

During this period unions were organized along craft lines. In the building trade, for example, carpenters would belong to one union, bricklayers to another union and plasterers to yet another union. This often led to rivalries between the unions and problems during strikes when one union demanded that the others honour their picket lines. Another difficulty was that most members of the craft unions were not in favour of organizing the unskilled workers, and when labourers went on strike the skilled workers often would not support their demands.

The polarization between skilled and unskilled workers was quite intense after 1900. "Organize the Unorganized": the slogan was a demand for unionization of unskilled workers. The fight was led by radical unions like the Industrial Workers of the World, nicknamed the Wobblies. By 1919 there were demands for "One Big Union" organized along industrial lines, where all the workers would be in one union, regardless of their skill. The craft unions, made up of skilled workers, liked the status quo and saw industrial unions as a threat. This split led to serious problems in the mass production industries, like steel and automobiles, industries that were growing rapidly in the early decades of the twentieth century.

All of these splits and antagonisms existed in the Hamilton trade union movement, but unlike other centres, union members and unorganized workers were able to work together politically in the city. In 1906 Allan Studholm, a member of the stove-moulder's union, was first elected to the Ontario provincial legislature and held the seat for three terms. By 1919 the Independent Labour Party had been formed in Canada and Hamilton elected three ILP members to the provincial legislature. They became part of Ontario's Farm/Labour government. The Independent Labour Party also made major gains in Hamilton's municipal government.

Hamilton unions were growing, but organizing efforts in the steel mills remained difficult. Steel is a mass-production industry. Most of the workers were unskilled labourers and had no union to represent them. There was a union that organized the skilled and some semi-skilled workers in the industry, which set a scale of pay for skilled jobs. It was called the Amalgamated Association of Iron, Steel and Tin Workers of North America, or the AA. A number of the workers at Stelco joined the AA in 1919 but in that same year the union went out on strike in fifty cities in the United States. The strike was crushed by a combination of strike-breakers and stubborn management that refused to recognize the union.

Originally there were three AA lodges organized in Stelco, but by the early 1920s only the lodge in the sheet mill existed. The company resisted recognizing the union and refused to negotiate with it, but they agreed to pay the union scale to the sheet mill workers, to let the union collect dues and post their notices in the mill. What emerged in the sheet mill was a type of shop floor militancy. If there was a problem, "tongs were banged, the whistle blown, the mill stopped rolling, the men marched to the office, and as a general rule appropriate changes were made."[6]

The wages paid by Stelco were better than those in most other industries, but there were huge problems in Hamilton's steel mills. Prior to the First World War there had been high immigration into Canada, and Stelco hired many Italians and Eastern Europeans. A type of systematic discrimination emerged in the plant. The so-called "ethnic workers" did the hot and dangerous jobs and received the lowest pay. They had no job security and could be fired on the whim of a foreman. The better jobs were reserved for native-born Canadians and British immigrants. The foremen and management were almost always Protestants and many were members of the Masons. This pattern of discrimination existed up to the 1946 strike and beyond, and was one of the major grievances of the workers.

The steel industry is a 24-hour-a-day, seven-day-a-week, 365-days-a-year operation. Once the furnaces are heated up to the temperatures needed to smelt steel, they are kept at that temperature until they are shut down for maintenance. It is shift work. Through the 1920s the men worked ten- and twelve-hour shifts, seven days a week. Heavy labour was the rule, particularly in the "bull gangs" of unskilled workers. Physical fatigue was a part of every steelworker's life. In the summer the heat was particularly exhausting in some of the mills where high-temperature furnaces operated or when the men handled red-hot steel. Often workers collapsed from heat exhaustion. Safety was a major concern. In 1918, out of a workforce of 6,709 men, there were 33 fatal or permanently disabling accidents. It was, as one of the characters in *Glory Days* describes it, "like a war zone."

And yet there was pride in being a Hamilton steelworker. The men who laboured in the mills considered themselves a "tough breed" who knew how to survive. The nature of the work crews, the type of work and even its dangers drew men together into close bonds of friendship and loyalty to each other. Leaders, particularly in the era before the union was established, were looked up to, because workers knew that they were putting their own jobs on the line for their workmates. Those types of social relationships build the solidarity that is essential for unions.

The Depression

Stelco employment in the 1920s averaged about 6,000 workers. It was the biggest and most important employer in the city, and the company had become essential in the growing industrial expansion of Canada. Stelco's steel was used in a wide variety of products, but much of its success was in producing steel for the growing automobile industry.

The stock market crash of 1929 and the Depression that resulted was a disaster for the company and the city. Hamilton's economy was reliant on heavy industry and the city suffered more than most Ontario centres. There were a number of plant closings, many factories cut back and the population of the city shrank. The two big steel plants, Stelco and Dofasco, operated at 40 to 50 per cent capacity. There were layoffs, reduced hours and wages.

Industries even today tend to be segregated along gender lines and that was even more common in the era prior to the Second World War. Industries like steel, that depended on male workers, were particularly hard hit in the Depression, but those that hired primarily women, like textiles, clothing and food processing, continued to work at or near capacity levels. The difficulty was that women's wages were about half of men's wages. In the Depression many Hamilton families survived on the wages of women and the occasional work the men could pick up.

Working-class Hamilton families experienced years of hardship and even serious deprivation. Welfare, or relief as it was called, was the last desperate resort of the unemployed. In 1933, the depths of the Depression, almost 25 per cent of Hamilton families were on relief; even this underestimates the need. Single men were not eligible for support. Many were forced to leave home to "ride the rails" across Canada looking for work.

In time, resentment against the welfare system grew. The city employed thirty-one welfare investigators whose job was to ensure that recipients followed the rules. Applicants had to go to the welfare office on Victoria Avenue North to get their welfare allowance. Almost every day a line formed that went out into the parking lot. When recipients finally got into the building they had to sit in every chair in the room until they had their turn to talk to the welfare officer. Investigators made surprise home visits to make sure that recipients did not drink alcohol or waste money. Physically fit men were required to work for a number of days every month on municipal projects like the Botanical Gardens and new roads.

The growing anger at the welfare system and the loss of jobs was turned against government and translated into support for political parties that advocated change. The Communist Party, active across Canada since the early 1920s, were very well organized, with a group of young men and women dedicated to "organizing the working class." The CCF, the Co-operative Commonwealth Federation, forerunner of the NDP, was founded in 1933. This left-wing parliamentary party had many Hamilton supporters. There was active competition between the two parties. Political rallies were common in Woodward Park at Barton and Sherman Streets. There were welfare marches in the city and agitation for jobs.[7]

The Depression also had an impact on the development of the union at Stelco. The AA lodge continued in the sheet mill until 1932, but it then lost its charter because there were only three dues-paying members. Wages sank even further after the charter was lost, and it was some months before the sheet mill workers realized that they were being paid below the AA rates. After angry meetings between the management and the men, wages of the sheet mill workers were increased by ten per cent, but the men were not satisfied. In 1934 they began to organize into a group they called the "Steelworkers Union."

At first the union accomplished little, and it looked as if the whole effort might collapse. A new executive took over the union and began to negotiate with the company. When no agreement was reached, in May 1935 the sheet mill workers struck. The men mounted picket lines twenty-four hours a day and the whole department was solid. After two weeks on the picket line the company offered a wage increase but no union recognition. There was opposition, but the majority of the sheet mill men voted to accept the offer.

This effort by the sheet mill workers at Stelco followed the pattern of unionization across North America. Other than the tradesmen, the sheet mill men were the most skilled workers in the plant, and the company could not easily replace them. These workers had another advantage. Sheet steel was sold mainly to the automobile industry, the best and steadiest customer that Stelco had in the 1930s. The company could not afford to lose any orders for sheet steel.

But as it happened, at the exact same time that the sheet mill workers were organizing, changes were happening in the trade union movement that would have a decisive influence on the growth and development of unions at Stelco. There had long been demands to organize workers into industrial unions, rather than organizing along craft lines. In 1935 a number of unions led by John L. Lewis, from the United Mine Workers, established the CIO, Committee for Industrial Organization. The CIO advocated industrial unions.

During these years the mass production industries such as steel, automobile, electric appliances, rubber, pulp and paper were growing rapidly. The vast majority of the workers in these industries were unskilled or semi-skilled labourers who received low wages. The CIO set out to organize them.

In the United States the CIO met with almost immediate success. American labour legislation had been changed to encourage unionization and the workers and their unions responded with a series of recognition strikes that changed industrial relations in that country. The Flint, Michigan sit-down strike of early 1937 was the most dramatic of these strikes. The workers occupied the factory and defied the law, the company and the police. By February they had forced General Motors, the largest company in the United States, to recognize the union. This agreement granted instant legitimacy and transformed the United Automobile workers into a large, powerful union.

Change in the steel industry in the United States was almost as dramatic. The CIO established the Steel Workers Organizing Committee (SWOC) and by late 1936 they had thousands of members. Then in March 1937, weeks after the successful conclusion to the Flint sit-down strike, John L. Lewis negotiated an agreement with U.S. Steel, the largest steel company in the country, for a ten-cent-an-hour wage increase, a forty-hour week and union recognition.

In Canada, efforts to organize the mass production industries took much longer, but the dramatic successes of the union organizing drives in the United States served as an example to Canadian unions and workers alike. In April 1937 the autoworkers in the Oshawa General Motors plant went on strike, but it ended with only a partial success. The leaders of Canadian industry were determined to keep unions out of their plants, and the legislation governing union activity was restrictive. Organizing in the Canadian steel industry was very slow. The first real success was in Cape Breton Island, when 2,900 workers at Dosco got union recognition in 1938, but in the big Hamilton steel plants, organizing efforts were frustrated.

A small group of Stelco workers followed all of these developments closely. On June 21, 1936, eighteen workers became charter members of Lodge 1005 of the Steel Workers Organizing Committee. The leadership of this fledgling union came primarily from the sheet mill but other workers were drawn into the struggle. Their resolve was to form an industrial union that would represent all Stelco workers.

Workers flocked to unions in the latter part of the 1930s, for a number of different reasons. Poverty and low wages were certainly prime motivations, as was the extreme insecurity caused by the Depression. Growing political awareness was another reason. But perhaps more than any single factor, unions grew because of the way that workers were treated.

Today it is almost hard to imagine the autocratic management style of companies in the 1930s. A big industrial concern like Stelco was a hierarchical world with senior management remote and isolated from manual workers. The middle managers such as the mill superintendents wielded great power, but many of the foremen were tyrants who preyed on the workers.

In *Glory Days*, Hugh Hilton, Stelco's president, gives Reg and Billy a lecture on what he expects of his foremen.

HILTON The job of my foremen is to make sure the employees work hard for this company. It's not easy. I run a steel mill, not a girl's school. Get this straight! I built this company. I redesigned this plant from top to bottom and finally got it running profitably. Do you think I'm going to lose it all to a bunch of complainers and whiners?

It's tough in this mill, and I expect the men who work here to be as tough as the steel they are producing. Do you understand?

Unskilled workers had no job security and could be fired on a moment's notice. Prejudice and favouritism were the rule rather than the exception. But the most grating of all to the men was that they were often forced to pay bribes to the foremen just to keep their jobs. Workers found it demeaning and humiliating and turned to unions as a way to gain justice.

War

What began to change all of this was the Second World War. Shortly after Canada entered the war in September 1939 the demand for steel rose dramatically as the company received orders for war materials. Many Stelco workers left to join the armed services and the company hired many new employees. Soon there was a labour shortage in Hamilton. Economic conditions swung from depression to boom times almost overnight, and nowhere was there a more serious labour shortage than in the steel mills.

These improved economic conditions strengthened the negotiating power of the unions. The threat of being fired for union activity lessened. Workers were in demand and could always get other employment. The company, realizing that they had to try to head off the grievances of the workers if they were to stop the efforts of the union organizers, set up a Stelco Works Council made up of an equal number of managers and elected workers. After a time the union activists took over the Works Council and the company abandoned this attempt to stop the union organizing drive.

The members of Lodge 1005 pushed aggressively to gain union recognition. They distributed leaflets and put up stickers in the plant on furnaces and notice boards. In November 1939, just months after the war had started, Tom McClure, the union president, wrote to Hilton asking for union recognition. A blistering reply was received.

> So long as the government of the province and the federal government are not the subject of control of any foreign power, this company declines to negotiate with any organization with communistic associations and supported by U.S. funds in any endeavour to secure control over its employees.[8]

The threat of communism and foreign influence was often used by Hilton in the mounting war of words between the union and the company. There was an element of truth in the accusation. Communists were active in 1005, but there were many members of other political parties. This rhetoric about radicals was more a reflection of the fear shared by Hilton and many other industrial leaders that unions were going to take over the management of their companies, an objective that was never part of the union strategy.

As the war ground on, the labour shortage crisis increased. Women were hired in many departments at Stelco, and men and women were recruited from across Canada to take jobs in the steel mills. The output of Stelco doubled and tripled, profits rose, and still the company could barely keep up with the demand for steel.

In the latter part of the war the federal government became increasingly involved in all aspects of the economy in order to ensure that output remained high for the wartime economy and that inflation was under control. This led to wage and price controls and restrictions on the movement of labour. Canadian unions were very unhappy about this because it harmed their ability to get better wages and working conditions for their members. On February 1, 1943 workers at Dosco in Nova Scotia and Algoma in Sault Ste. Marie went on an illegal strike. They only went back to work when the government promised to change the labour legislation.

This promise was finally kept in January 1944 when the federal government enacted P.C. 1003. This was the first major change to Canada's labour legislation since 1907. The order in council gave workers the right to organize, certification of bargaining units and compulsory collective bargaining.

In the meantime, Local 1005 had applied for official certification by the labour court in October 1943. (SWOC formally became the United

Steelworkers of America in 1942 and Lodge 1005 became Local 1005.) When this case was heard before the labour court the company argued that only a handful of Stelco workers were actually members of the union. The Steelworkers admitted that at the time of the proceedings the union local only had 259 dues-paying members and the highest they ever had was 771, but the unionists argued that this was because the company would not allow automatic dues check-off of all members. The court ordered a vote of Stelco employees, which was held on the February 2, 1944. Out of the 3,781 ballots cast, 2,461 were in favour of the Steelworkers becoming the official bargaining agent. The official order of certification was issued on April 6, 1944.

The time seemed right to establish a system of collective bargaining at Stelco, but it did not happen. Hugh Hilton, the president of Stelco, was adamant that a union not be established in his plant. An uneasy peace emerged between the union and the company in the concluding days of the war. The production of steel remained high, the union was active and yet the company stalled any attempts by Local 1005 to collectively bargain. Union recognition was destined to wait until the boys came home from the war.

Most Stelco workers and their families were determined to get union recognition. They had suffered the deprivations of the Depression and the hardships of war. They were fed up with existing conditions in the steel mills and demanded changes. This is how the characters in *Glory Days* expressed their frustrations:

> **NATE** *(to his wife, ROSE)* This is important! There is nothin' that's goin' to make me back down from this strike. Nothin'!
>
> **BILLY** *(waving his fist)* I'm just hurtin' for it, know what I mean. Things have gotta change!
>
> **LOUIS** I did five years of service for this country. Nobody's gonna call me a Wop no more!
>
> **BILLY** We want [a union] so bad we're ready to bleed for it!

The Prelude

The Second World War ended in August 1945. Almost immediately pressure was put on labour leaders across the county to improve wages and working conditions. In Local 1005 union activity became intense. Larry

Sefton, a new Hamilton organizer, was brought in, and elections in the Local resulted in a new President, Reg Gardiner. These two men became the key organizers of the local union.

The company prepared for labour trouble. Leaders of the Canadian business community were concerned that there would be a return of Depression conditions after the war and they resisted union organizing because it would drive up costs. But the key reason for the resistance to union organization was ideology. Many business leaders feared that unionization would lead to left wing or even communistic leadership of their workers, and they were determined to stop this rising red tide. One of the strongest and most vocal of the anti-union business leaders was Hugh Hilton, the president of Stelco.

Hilton was an engineer who had worked in the steel industry all of his adult life. He had joined Stelco in 1919 and by the 1930s he was the day-to-day manager of operations. He is credited with the reorganization of the giant steel plant and making it profitable. In 1944 he was appointed president. Hilton considered himself to be a tough steelworker who dealt with workers "man to man." Associates described him as an intense man, not given to small talk but capable of inspiring loyalty and respect. He was a traditionalist who believed that the only way to run a steel mill was by an authoritarian chain of command. Hilton opposed unions because he felt that they threatened management's ability to control the workplace and in time that would lead to a disaster for the company.[9]

By 1946 the Steelworkers were officially recognized as the bargaining agent for three of the four basic steel producers in the country: Stelco, Algoma and Dosco.[10] The union established a set of contract demands to take to all of the companies and began negotiating early in the year. From the beginning the Steelworkers knew that the most difficult of these contracts would be with Stelco. The company's anti-union reputation was well known, and Hugh Hilton's reputation was legendary, but they also knew that the Stelco negotiations were the most important. The company was a pacesetter in the industry. It was the largest steel producer in the country and paid the best wages. An agreement between the Steelworkers and Stelco would set a pattern that would be used in the steel industry and other manufacturing companies. It would be a moral victory that would help the union in their organizing efforts across the country.

The Steelworkers had four basic demands. They called for a 19-cent-an-hour wage increase—which would raise the minimum wage to 84 cents an hour—a forty-hour work week, two weeks paid vacation after five years service and a union shop with automatic check-off of union dues. Of these demands union security and dues check-off was the most important. This would signal that the union was finally accepted by the company.

When the negotiations began in the spring of 1946 the company made it clear that they would oppose the union demands. Stelco offered only a 5-cent-an-hour increase, knowing this would be totally unacceptable to the union, and they opposed union security provision of dues check-off. Attitudes of union members hardened. In the United States a strike ended in February 1946 with an increase in minimum wage to 97 cents an hour and union security with check off. As well, the Canadian federal government allowed the steel companies to raise the price of steel by $5 a ton, but at the same time kept wartime controls over wages. In May the government announced that they would allow wages to increase by 10 cents an hour, but by that time it was totally unacceptable to the unions.

The Steelworkers knew that a strike was coming, and on May 11, Local 1005 took a vote of all Stelco workers, not just those who were members of the union, to see if they supported the Steelworkers demands. The result showed 3,114 in favour of striking, while only 80 were opposed.

The Steelworkers had set a strike deadline of July 15 if an agreement had not been reached. As the date approached the workers began to realize that the company was preparing in earnest for a strike. Iron ore, coal and other raw materials were being stockpiled. Stelco began bringing in food and bedding. A long stretch of land beside the water had been cleared and smoothed down. The yard crew realized that they had been building an aircraft landing strip. Even more ominous, early in July the company hired extra workers, many of whom were university and high school students. Finally the unionists understood that the company was planning to continue operating through the strike.

In a last effort to head off a strike, Charles Millard, the Canadian Steelworkers President, led a delegation of Local 1005 members to meet with Hugh Hilton in his office. The company president indicated that he intended to keep producing steel and would break the union. "I know that there are thousands of our employees who will not go out on strike," he told the delegation. Reg Gardiner, the 1005 President, replied with equal vehemence that he was sure that thousands would.[11] The two sides were at an impasse; a strike was inevitable.

Political leaders in Ottawa were very concerned about the impending strike. They feared that if the steel companies went on strike it would seriously damage the economy as the country changed from wartime to peacetime production. On July 11, just four days before the strike deadline, the federal cabinet issued an order in council placing the three steel companies under government trusteeship. Any worker refusing to work could be subject to a $20-a-day fine.

This put the union in a terrible quandary. If they defied the law their members could be subject to fines and possible imprisonment, but if they caved in and told their members to stay at work the union would be condemned as useless. [12] It would put back the organizing drive for years. There was no hesitation on the part of the union leaders. They condemned the government's action. Charles Millard said "the government is quite prepared to rush to the side of the employer." [13]

On Sunday, July 14, the evening before the strike deadline, the membership of Local 1005 gathered at the Playhouse Cinema on Sherman Avenue, close to the steel plant, to discuss what the union should do. It was hot and humid, and the old theatre was crammed with steelworkers. Inspiring speeches were given to rousing cheers. Suddenly the doors of the theatre opened, the crowd surged out onto the street and marched north to the Wilcox Gate. The strike was on!

Strike Lines are Drawn

In the summer of 1946 the City of Hamilton was virtually paralyzed with industrial strikes. On June 24, 1,500 Rubber Workers had struck Firestone, and on July 5, 4,000 United Electrical Workers in the city's Westinghouse plants followed them. Workers at the *Spectator* also went out, but the newspaper continued to publish. When Stelco workers went out on strike on July 15, one out of every eleven workers in the city was out on strike and another 2,000 were soon laid off. But where no one crossed the lines of Westinghouse and Firestone, on the Stelco picket lines the very existence of the Steelworkers' Union was being challenged.

Hilton was going to continue producing steel during the strike. If the company could deliver that steel to its customers they could ignore the union and starve the strikers into submission. In time the workers would be forced to go back to work under the company's terms and the union would be finished. The strike was a struggle for the very existence of the Steelworkers Union.

As the strike approached, the workers had to choose sides between the employer and the union. For many it was not an easy decision. Memories of the Depression were still fresh in the minds of everyone. Stelco paid higher than normal wages and to make it attractive for workers to stay in the plant, the company increased wages by 10 cents an hour and offered all strike breakers triple time because they would be forced to stay in the plant 24 hours a day.

There were huge risks in going out on strike. The union had no strike fund and strikers and their families would have to survive on their savings. If the strike were lost, the union leadership would be fired and the jobs of anyone actively participating in the strike would be at risk. All the union could offer was the promise of a better future, and yet despite the risks, the majority of the workers chose to go on strike. The union had convinced most Stelco workers that if they could establish the Steelworkers Union it would be of lasting benefit to them all.

It was the backgrounds of workers that were the most important factor in determining what side of the struggle each of them supported. The strongest supporters were the so-called ethnic workers. The Italians, Ukrainians and Poles solidly supported the strike. Discriminated against for years, locked in the heavy, dirty, unskilled jobs, they felt they had nothing to lose by going out on strike. The Canadian-born were split, but most supported the strike. It was the English, Scots and Irish who tended to be the strikebreakers. They had the best jobs and they feared that they would lose their special treatment if they went on strike.

All of the foremen and an undetermined number of workers stayed in the plant once the strike started. There was another large group of strike-breakers, the McMaster University and high school students the company had hired in the build-up to the strike. Most stayed in the plant once the strike started.

After the first day of the strike, the war of words—claims and counter-claims—began, with both sides participating. Hugh Hilton told the press that 2,000 men were in the plant and they were continuing to produce steel. The union countered by saying that, out of the workforce of 4,800 production workers, only 800 were still in the plant along with 400 foremen. A massive union picket line surrounded the giant industrial complex, but ominously the picketers watched as smoke billowed out of the stacks. Steel was being produced. If it were delivered to Stelco customers the union was doomed.

The press was drawn to this strike because of the dramatic nature of the conflict. They reported that the men inside the plant were very comfortable. They slept in double-decker bunks and ate in one of five dining rooms. All of the strikebreakers could contact their families by phone and the company provided a "family information office." Morale was very high, according to the newspapers.

The strikers quickly retaliated. Homes of the strikebreakers were painted with large letters spelling out "SCAB." A few days after the strike started the company complained that strikers had climbed over the fences and had pulled wires out of cars and put sand in gas tanks. The union denied any involvement.

On the night of July 16–17, the company tried to run a train with twenty freight cars carrying steel through the picket lines at the Stelco main gate. As the train paused at the plant gate, three hundred men "armed with pick handles and rubber hoses attacked the picketers," driving them back with bricks and rocks. The company men rushed to remove the ties blocking the train tracks and pry open the spiked switches. The picketers shouted for help. Strikers from the other gates ran to their aid. The battle raged, with bricks and stones raining down on each side until the Hamilton police arrived in four cruisers to restore order. Half an hour after it began the company men gave up and retreated back into the plant.[14]

A few days later there was a similar incident. Most railway workers had promised not to handle "scab steel," but when a TH&B (Toronto, Hamilton and Buffalo) train approached the Burlington Street gate, preparing to cross the picket line, the picketers massed on the line and made it clear to the railway men that if they attempted to cross there would be retaliation. The train stopped while the railway men considered their options, and then retreated. There would not be another attempt to cross the picket line by train for the duration of the strike.

This was a key battle of the strike. If the company could run trains through the picket line and deliver steel to their customers then the strike could be broken. But if they couldn't get through the picket line, the company could make all the steel they liked and it would do no good. With access to their customers cut off, it was Stelco that was in trouble. All they could do was appeal to the politicians to open the picket lines.

The Politicians Enter the Strike

Hamilton is an industrial city, and for many years workers supported and elected politicians sympathetic to unions. Their strongest supporter at the time of the strike was Mayor Sam Lawrence. Lawrence, an English immigrant, was a stonemason by trade and a lifelong trade unionist. He started his political career as a Hamilton alderman in 1922 and then won a position on the Board of Control. He spent one term in the provincial legislature and when he was defeated he returned to Hamilton city politics. He was elected mayor in 1943.

Four days before the strike began, the mayor took part in a rally to support the strikers, which concluded with a huge demonstration in Woodlands Park. He used the opportunity to explain where his loyalties lay. Declaring that he was a "labour man first and a chief magistrate second," he went on to say he was 100 per cent behind the workers in their struggle.[15]

The federal government had seized control of the steel industry a few days before the strike began. The question was, what were they going to do now that the workers were on strike, defying the law? The Mackenzie King government was in an obvious quandary. They could send in the police, but could the police actually force the workers back to work? Using violence against the strikers would be wildly unpopular with the whole population, but could the government simply ignore this blatant violation of the law?

As a tactic to divert attention and to make it appear that the government was doing something, King ordered an all-party parliamentary inquiry to investigate the steel strike. The first witness was Charles Millard, the Canadian director of the Steelworkers. He accused the government of attempting to subvert the collective bargaining process. Then he turned his guns on Hugh Hilton and Stelco, saying that the company had been planning for months to subvert the collective bargaining process and break the strike.

When Hilton appeared before the committee three days later he was equally provocative. "We… protest against the policy of coercion and violation of the law which has prevailed since the CIO started operations." He concluded, "I am sure the sentiments of right-thinking Canadians will be that the government is derelict in its duty unless it requires that the union obey the laws that allow us to produce steel."[16]

Other politicians picked up this issue of "law and order." Nora-Frances Henderson, a Hamilton Controller, sided with Hugh Hilton and Stelco. She deplored the "state of lawlessness" of the city and denounced the mayor for his support of the strikers. On August 2, she marched to the picket line, bringing photographers and reporters in tow, and demanded access to the plant. The picture of her small figure surrounded by big steelworkers was on the front pages of newspapers across the country. But the picketers, instead of denying her entry, courteously ushered her through the lines.

When she reappeared, Nora-Frances, as she was known by everyone, argued strongly for the full imposition of law. "This form of picketing is illegal," she said. "There is intimidation and threats of violence.... What burns me up is that 2,700 men inside the plant are denied free access to the municipality... I will not bow to mob rule." She went on to call for a Board of Control meeting to deal with "the state of lawlessness in Hamilton." [17] On August 9, a city council meeting was held to deal with the issue. Thousands of strikers and their supporters showed up at city hall only to find that the seats of the chamber were taken by Stelco office personnel. A huge pro-strike crowd gathered on the street to hear the outcome. The most important moment of the debate came when the Police Chief claimed there were no major problems on the picket lines. After four hours of debate the council voted 9 to 7 that provincial police were not needed.

Sam Lawrence and labour supporters were cheered when they appeared on the street but when Nora-Frances came out the crowd became unruly. They sang "We'll Hang Nora-Frances to the Sour Apple Tree." When she got to her car it looked for a moment that it might be turned over by the crowd, but union men intervened and she drove away peacefully.

This fueled the claim of lawlessness, and led to more demands for police protection. The Steelworkers Union blamed the Communists, claiming that they themselves had played no part in the incident. The police chief issued a stern warning stating that violence would not be tolerated. Tension was high. It seemed like any moment things could erupt into violence.

The Siege of Stelco

The picket line around the huge company property was maintained twenty-four hours a day. Most of the picketers were Stelco workers but they were supplemented by striking unionists from Westinghouse and Firestone. Restlessly the picketers moved along the fence line watching for any movement inside the plant, ready to spring into action at a moment's notice. At night, union commandos with blackened faces would slip through the fences and carry out acts of sabotage.

The company had been preparing for the strike for months. Pat Kelly, a prominent public relations expert, was hired to advise Hugh Hilton; Kelly soon became the chief company tactician. Unlike Hilton, Kelly accepted that unions were here to stay; the role of companies should be to "educate the union leadership on how to get along with business."[18] Kelly also understood that if the company were to win this strike, they would have to have the support of the public.

When the strike started, Kelly moved into the Royal Connaught Hotel in downtown Hamilton and kept in touch with every aspect of the company's operations by telephone. Hilton came to rely on him so much, that within a couple of weeks he moved into Kelly's suite and the two of them managed the company during the strike from this command post. There Kelly wrote press releases and radio speeches, coached Hilton in his presentation to the Commons Standing Committee on Industrial Relations and wrote his brief.

Kelly rented a storefront on Barton Street and organized a Family Services Bureau to help the strikebreakers maintain easy contact with their families. A staff of thirty ex-servicemen manned the bureau. They shepherded the scabs in and out of the plant so they could see their families. Usually they were taken out by a converted tug across the bay but often the strikebreakers would slip through the picket lines in the dead of night.

Radio was an important medium during this era. CHML in Hamilton, with the largest audience in the city, reported regularly on the strike. After the Steelworkers bought time on CHML and union leaders made regular broadcasts, Kelly insisted that Stelco should have equal time on the airwaves. The station agreed, and aired a daily program titled "Canada's Biggest Family," broadcasting music, skits and speeches from the strike-bound plant. The strikebreakers called the broadcasts "HMCS Scab," and named themselves the "Fraternal Order of Scabs."

The union also mounted a sophisticated public relations campaign. Murray Cotterill, a young, aggressive trade unionist and CCF leader, organized this effort. The Steelworkers used radio extensively but they also made themselves available to comment to the press at any time. The picket line was regularly leafleted with union news and groups of strikers and their families were sent to the city centre to distribute their flyers. The union message was unrelenting. The strike would not end until union demands were met.

On the picket line the strikers harassed the strikebreakers at every opportunity. When they learned that the scabs were sleeping in metal sheds not far from the line, the union set up loudspeakers blaring union messages to disturb the scabs' sleep. One group of strikers rigged up a giant slingshot to hurl stones at the sheds while others whiled away the hours on the picket line by hurling rocks at the metal roofs. Fights and skirmishes broke out whenever scabs were caught going through the fences.

The wives, mothers and girlfriends of the strikers made sandwiches for the picketers and organized the welfare committee to make sure that no family of a striker went hungry. Farmers donated fruit and vegetables to the families. Many women and children came to walk with their men on the picket line. On Fridays the Italian women made and served spaghetti for all of the picketers and their families. *The Globe and Mail* of August 28 carried this account of the mood on the picket line.

> "Out on Burlington Street, on the patchy gray grass, sit sympathizers. They sit along curbs, smoking, chatting. Pickets join them in their spells off duty. Many of the watchers are women. Women come and go all day long, most of them accompanied by children, down to visit their dads on the line." [19]

Every evening a large crowd of spectators gathered at the Wilcox Gate on Burlington Street. There was entertainment to keep up the strikers' spirits. Pete Seager, the famous folk singer, travelled to Hamilton to perform on the picket line. Whipper Billy Watson gave a demonstration of wrestling techniques. The Christmas Sisters, three women whose husbands and brothers worked in the plant, sang songs for the strikers. A favourite was the "Scab Song," which the sisters wrote about the strike and performed to the cheers of the strikers and their families. [20] Spirits were high. At times it was almost festive on the picket line.

The Stelco plant is located on the water's edge of Hamilton Bay. The strikers could stop strikebreakers trying to cross the picket line, but it was much more difficult to patrol the company docks on the water. Shortly after the strike started, Stelco began running boats across the bay, and this soon became the major way that the company brought in strikebreakers, food, equipment and raw materials.

On August 12, 3,000 tons of billets, rods and coils were loaded aboard the Canada Steamship Lines ship *Selkirk* and sailed for Montreal. There was panic. If Stelco could deliver its steel to customers the Steelworkers could lose the strike. But two days later the Lachine Canal workers announced that they refused to handle "scab steel." The crisis was averted.

The Steelworkers Union recognized that they had to plug this waterfront hole in their picket line. They bought a motor launch from a Hamilton bootlegger, rechristened it *Whisper*, and recruited a number of strikers into the "union navy." The *Whisper* was powered by two huge Chrysler engines that could push its speed up to forty miles an hour, making it the fastest boat on the bay. Day and night the *Whisper* patrolled the harbour. Whenever a company boat approached the Stelco docks, the *Whisper* would speed in and try to swamp the company boat with its huge wake. There were fights whenever the crew surprised a company boat loading supplies. When the *Whisper* came close to the company docks, scabs would bombard it with chunks of slag. Ultimately the Hamilton harbour police impounded the *Whisper* and members of the crew were fined, but the boat had served its purpose in harassing the company and keeping up union morale.

Perhaps the strangest incident of the strike was a battle in the skies. The company had a plane which could land on an airstrip inside the plant. The plane was used to ferry company officials over the picket line. On July 30, the union hired their own aircraft and one of the union men, an RCAF veteran, flew over the plant and scattered leaflets, urging the scabs to abandon the company and join the strike. Suddenly the company plane, piloted by another RCAF veteran, raced in, forcing the union plane into "a violent and undignified climb." (*Op. Cit.*, Kilbourn, *The Elements Combined*, p. 194.) The dogfight continued for several minutes, watched by strikers and scabs on the ground, before the two broke off the engagement and returned to their respective airports.

Threat of the Law

As the strike dragged on through the hot summer of 1946, tensions rose and tempers flared. The company felt frustrated. Hugh Hilton complained to the press that laws were being violated and the company and its loyal employees were not being given adequate protection. Pressure mounted on the union. Members were suffering financial hardships. There were threats that mortgages and loans would be called because strikers could not keep up with their payments. An increasing number of strikers stopped coming to the picket line, either because they were discouraged or because they had to take part-time work to help pay their mounting bills.

There were splits within the union. The CCF group that held the leadership positions in the Steelworkers urged their members to hold fast, telling them that in time the strike would force the company to give in. The Communists still had influence in the union local and they urged more radical action. There was a mounting feeling that something dramatic had to happen or the strike would be lost.

Incidents on the picket line continued. By mid-August the once-solid picket lines were beginning to show signs of weakening. The company, sensing this, began to run trucks through the line. In retaliation the union massed strikers at the road entrances. Cars were overturned to block the gates. Trucks were stopped, engine wires pulled out, fights escalated.

Nora-Frances Henderson had lost the initial vote at City Council on August 9 to bring in additional police but she did not give up. Several times she talked on the radio and to the press about the mounting lawlessness of the picket line. "Serious events are taking place which are not only disturbing the peaceful and secure life of our citizens, but which constitute the gravest threat to the constitution."[21] She described beatings of strike-breakers in detail and concluded that the police could not maintain order.

Members of the federal government and business leaders voiced concern about the impact of the steel strike on the Canadian economy. Many companies were complaining that they might have to shut down their operations because they could not get steel. There was fear that if the price of steel went up it would fuel inflation, affecting the entire economy. The pressure on the government to act mounted, but there was no consensus on what to do.

On August 21 there was a skirmish on the picket line between sixty Hamilton policemen and about one thousand strikers. Afterwards the police chief said that law and order could not be maintained without reinforcements. At the police commission meeting two days later a resolution was put forward asking for reinforcements. Mayor Sam Lawrence opposed the resolution, but it passed, and the request was sent to the provincial government. Immediately the Attorney General of Ontario announced that he was sending 250 OPP officers to Hamilton.

Shortly afterwards the federal government announced that they were matching this number by sending 250 members of the RCMP.

The situation on the picket line was tense as the extra police moved into the city. The officers were billeted in wartime service houses in the city's working class north end. Kitchen staff at the barracks refused to work for them. Waitresses in neighbourhood restaurants refused to serve them if they were in uniform. Everyone predicted that these outside police officers would soon be ordered to attack the strikers and open the picket line.

Then, on August 26, came a moment of great drama. As a show of solidarity a group from the Studebaker plant organized a march in support of the Stelco strikers. The call went out, and they were joined by delegations from churches, farmers and students, and most importantly, veterans. Decommissioned from the armed forces less than a year before, hundreds joined in the march. By the time the procession reached the Stelco main gate, 10,000 people were in the parade.

The OPP and RCMP reinforcements had just arrived in the city. The strikers widely believed that this would be the moment they would choose to attack, but the march concluded without incident. The politicians and police recognized that to attack the march—filled with veterans who so recently had put their lives on the line for their country—would have been political suicide.

And the strike wore on. In late August a meeting was held between federal government officials and the union in Ottawa to discuss new terms for a settlement, but it was rejected out of hand as simply reiterating proposals made before the strike started. Then, on September 18, Hugh Hilton made a personal appeal to the strikers by sending letters directly to their homes. He offered a minor wage increase but rejected union security, the key union demand. He wrote: "Most emphatically the company will not be a party to any arrangement which might result in employees being compelled to pay union dues against their wishes." [22]

The Settlement and Beyond

By mid September it appeared that the strike would never be settled. The two sides were as far apart as ever, particularly on the issue of union security. Hilton was intractable, and the union leadership was just as determined to stick by their demands. Both sides felt they had to have a victory or all of the hardships and sacrifices would result in nothing.

In the end it was pressure from the federal government that led to the settlement. By this time the shortage of steel was having a serious effect on the Canadian economy. Workers were being laid off in secondary industries. Even more serious, union leaders across the country had begun to talk of a general strike if there was not a favourable settlement between Stelco and the Steelworkers. Government leaders knew that if a recession was to be avoided, and the overheated political tempers calmed, the steel strike must be settled.

Various meetings occurred behind closed doors in an effort to settle the strike. Years later Pat Kelly admitted that he arranged for Hugh Hilton to have a private dinner with Charles Millard. It must have been a strange meal. Hilton's only comment about the event was his shock at discovering that Millard was a teetotaller,[23] strange behaviour to the hard drinking steel company president.

Thomas Rahilly, a leading industrialist, offered to be an intermediary between the union and the company but first he asked for reassurance. "Are you a socialist?" he asked Charles Millard. "With all my heart," Millard replied. "But I am a democrat. I don't think we'll see it in my time."[24]

Within a few days Millard met with the government controller in Montreal who had the consent of the company to make a new offer. They agreed to terms in fifteen minutes. The settlement gave an immediate increase in wages of 13 cents an hour and an additional five cents before the end of the year. Other issues were to be settled later. On the key issue of union security the final agreement provided for a voluntary check-off of union dues if fifty plus one per cent of the employees agreed within thirty days. It took only four days to reach the required number. The Steelworkers and Local 1005 were finally on a firm footing.

On October 3, the picket lines around the huge Stelco plant were finally lifted: the siege of Stelco was over. The strikebreakers who had stayed in the plant came out through the gates, met by the jeers and taunts of the strikers. For years many strikers refused to talk to the scabs, and in some cases the rift never healed.

The Stelco strike of 1946 remains a watershed event in the history of the Canadian trade union movement and the city of Hamilton. From 1945 to 1948 a series of strikes established industrial unions on a firm footing, and one of the most important was the '46 Stelco strike. With union security and dues check-off, the unions had the financial and organizational power to provide real and meaningful protection to their members.

In the 1940s and '50s it was the mass production industries like steel and auto that led the unionizing drives, but since the 1960s, union protection has extended to cover government workers and a wide variety of other industries. Today unions represent a little more than 30% of the non-agricultural workers of Canada. This is substantially higher than the United States, although not as high as most European countries.

The play *Glory Days* describes Stelco in the 1930s and early '40s as a workplace rank with discrimination and favouritism. The workers lived under a form of tyranny where the boss was king and their needs and wishes were simply disregarded. That system existed not because Hugh Hilton was a terrible man. There is much to admire about Hilton and other leaders of industry of the time. But the common belief of management of the day was that workers needed to be disciplined and tough foremen were an absolute necessity if companies were to survive. Under that system, workers had no power and no means to be able to struggle against that tyranny. The greatest achievement of unions is that they gave workers the means to challenge this system, and this led to a change of attitudes to the point where today no company, unionized or non-unionized, would dare treat their workforce in such autocratic and discriminatory ways.

It is common to hear people say that unions were once necessary but they have become too powerful and they are not needed today. Nothing could be further from the truth. Unions are practical grassroots organizations that provide security, protection and rights for millions of Canadians. They are part of the democratic structure of our society and should be celebrated for all they have accomplished. Billy concludes *Glory Days* with these lines:

> **BILLY** The '46 Stelco strike was a victory won on the picket line. It changed the way workers were treated in this country… how people treated each other.

That is the legacy of the '46 Stelco strike.

• • •

Notes

[1] I have written about Stelco and the United Steelworkers in two previously published books.
Bill Freeman, *1005: Political Life in a Union Local,* (Toronto: James Lorimer & Company, Publishers, 1982) and
Bill Freeman, "Welfare Hamilton Style," in *Their Town: The Mafia, the Media and the Party Machine,* editors, Bill Freeman & Marsha Hewitt, (Toronto: James Lorimer & Company, Publishers, 1979).

[2] Today most of the iron ore used in the Hamilton mills comes from Labrador. The ore is smelted into pellets at Sept-Iles, Quebec and brought by ship up the St. Lawrence to Hamilton.

[3] William Kilbourn, *The Elements Combined: A History of the Steel Company of Canada,* (Toronto: Clarke Irwin, 1960) p. 49.

[4] Max Aitken took the profits he made in this merger and moved to England. There he became a Member of Parliament, influential in British politics and a newspaper magnate. In 1917 he was given a peerage and became known as Lord Beaverbrook. His influence on British politics continued until his death in 1964.

[5] *Op. cit.* Freeman, "Welfare Hamilton Style," p. 40.

[6] Tom McClure's notes, p. 2–3.

[7] For a discussion of the impact of the Depression on Hamilton, see Bill Freeman, *Hamilton: A People's History,* (Toronto: James Lorimer & Company, Publishers, 2001) p. 135–37.

[8] Letter from H.G. Hilton, vice-president of the Steel Company of Canada to Thomas W. McClure, president of Lodge 1005, 30 November 1939.

[9] *Op. cit., 1005: Political Life in a Union Local,* p. 49.

[10] The Steelworkers have made several attempts to organize Dofasco workers in Hamilton but have failed. Dofasco has a policy of matching the wage settlements agreed to by Stelco and Local 1005. They also have a generous employee stock option plan. These benefits have headed off unionization.

[11] *Op. cit., 1005: Political Life in a Union Local,* p. 53.

[12] The National Film Board of Canada, "Defying the Law," 1997. This film on the 1946 Stelco strike emphasizes that the workers were striking illegally. The film has strong visuals and it is highly recommended for anyone wanting to do further research on the '46 Stelco strike.

[13] *Op. cit., 1005: Political Life in a Union Local*, p. 54.

[14] *Ibid.*, p. 57.

[15] *Ibid.*, p. 59.

[16] *Ibid.*, p. 59–60.

[17] *Ibid.*, p. 61.

[18] "Interview with R.N. (Pat) Kelly, December 9, 1971." The character Olive Kelly, in *Glory Days*, is loosely based on Pat Kelly but is my fictional invention. The two characters, one real and one fictional, do, however, share certain points of view. Both felt that the best way to deal with workers' problems was to negotiate and try and meet their demands. Hilton, on the other hand, was anti-union both in real life and in the play.

[19] *The Globe and Mail*, August 28, 1946.

[20] The "Scab Song" that appears in *Glory Days* is an adaptation of the Christmas Sisters' song. The lyrics of the song were found in the archives without any music. Charles T. Cozens wrote new music for the play. It is preformed in the style of the McGuire Sisters, a musical group that was popular at the time of the strike.

[21] Nora-Frances Henderson, radio address CKOC, Hamilton, August 7, 1946.

[22] *Op. cit., 1005: Political Life in a Union Local*, p. 65.

[23] "Interview with R.N. (Pat) Kelly, December 9, 1971.

[24] *The Globe and Mail*, 7 August 1971.

***The Development of Music for the Stage Play* Glory Days**

In 1987, I was commissioned by Peter Mandia, Artistic Director and founder of Theatre Aquarius in Hamilton, Ontario, Canada to compose and produce specialized music and soundscapes for the dramatic play *Glory Days* by Bill Freeman.

After several meetings among Peter, Bill and myself, we discovered that the score should have several different layers to support the script. In particular, those layers and elements were to include period music (1940s), post-modern 20th century compositional techniques to create and personify Stelco the factory, a song about "scabs" and several union songs from the public domain such as "Solidarity Forever."

In addition, we desired to create a song about Stelco men, which would portray their sense of pride and their dedicated work ethics. Thus was born the "Song Of Steel." It is interesting to note that I arranged and produced the "Song Of Steel" in a contemporary pop style and the reason was to relate the struggle and sense of pride that the steel workers had in the 1940s to the modern day. In a sense, timeless.

Once the score was composed, it was pre-recorded and the resulting tracks were used in the live stage presentation.

I used many techniques to compose the score, one of which was particularly unique and exciting. I decided that in order to create a special soundscape for Stelco the Factory and give it a sense of being, I would embark on a guided tour of the factory itself with a Nagra tape deck in hand for the purpose of recording as many sounds as possible unique to the inner mechanism of a steel factory.

I contacted Stelco about the matter and was provided with a hard hat and an escort who took me into the bowels of the factory. Indeed it was an exciting experience. I was able to get very close to hammering anvils, trains, cranes, whistles and of course the open hearth and blast furnaces. I put the microphone as close as I dared, wishing to capture those noises that were the essence of the factory!

It proved to be quite successful. I captured a plethora of exciting sounds. But now, what was I to do with them?

Digital technology in the 1980s was in early stages. Nevertheless, I decided to download the taped information into an Akai 900 Sampler –

a musical instrument that sampled sounds and allowed one to edit them in many ways.

Once all of the information was transferred to the sampler, I was able to assign each sound to be accessed by a key on a MIDI keyboard. Simply, this allowed me to "play" the factory like a piano. From there, I was able to create the "Factory Overture" and subsequent soundscapes.

Glory Days was remounted at Theatre Aquarius in September 2006. Some of the original music was used and some new ideas were added. In particular, I developed an *a cappella* version of a union song entitled "Which Side Are You On?" to close both Act One and Act Two. This proved to be highly effective and quite moving.

As a composer, I have enjoyed contributing to this wonderful story of human courage, endurance and passion.

For more information on the music of *Glory Days* or to purchase this music, you may visit www.charlescozens.com

—Charles T. Cozens, Composer

Historical Photo Gallery

(for photo sources, please see page 148)

Stelco's enormous plant on Hamilton's waterfront grew slowly after the company was founded in the 1890s. This photo shows some of the mills in the 1920s.

The major products of Stelco were steel and pig iron but the plant also had mills where finished steel products were manufactured.

Molten steel being poured into molds during the1940s.
Long hours, heavy physical labour and unsafe working conditions characterized the steel industry in this period.

Sam Lawrence, the Mayor of Hamilton at the time of the '46 strike, was a strong unionist who supported the strikers. At a rally four days before the strike began he declared he was, "a union man first and a chief magistrate second."

During the '46 Stelco strike picketers sealed the plant gates. The company supplied the strike breakers inside the plant by boat across the bay. This is a photo of the union boat, the *Whisper* that harassed the company boats.

The Steelworkers Union hired an airplane to drop leaflets
to the scabs inside the plant and to pursue the company plane
that landed inside the grounds of the plant.

Nora-Frances Henderson, a City of Hamilton Controller at the time
of the strike, demanded that strike breakers be allowed through the picket line.
The strikers refused but they did allow her to cross the line
and visit the scabs inside the plant.

During the strike boredom was a problem for both the picketers and the scabs.

The scabs in the plant amused themselves by providing their own entertainment. The company broadcast a radio program from inside the plant featuring the strike breakers and attacking the union.

At the end of the strike the picket line was lifted and the strike breakers went home, but bitter feelings between the strikers and the scabs continued for years.

Glory Days was first produced by Theatre Aquarius at the Hamilton Place Studio Theatre from September 28 – October 22, **1988** with the following company:

Nate / Mayor Sam Lawrence	Victor Ertmanis
Rose / Nora-Frances Henderson	Diana Belshaw
Marie	Gina Wilkinson
Reg	Stephen Walsh
Alice	Norma Dell'Agnese
Louis / Kelly	John Pyper-Ferguson
Frank / Hilton	Harry Booker
Billy	Ronn Sarosiak

Directed by Peter Mandia
Set and Costumes Designed by Mary Jo Pollak
Lighting Designed by Paul Mathiesen
Stage Manager: Nancy Benedict
Assistant Stage Manager: Ross Gibaut
Composer/Music Director: Charles T. Cozens

• • •

Glory Days was subsequently remounted by Theatre Aquarius in the Irving Zucker Auditorium at the Dofasco Centre for the Arts from September 20 – October 7, **2006** with the following company:

Nate	Tim Campbell
Billy	Caden Douglas
Marie	Lina Giornofelice
Kelly / Nora-Frances Henderson	Kate Hennig
Reg	Ryan Hollyman
Rose	Tara Hughes
Frank / Sam Lawrence	George Masswohl
Louis	Paolo Mancini
Alice	Stephanie McNamara
Hilton and Tim Buck	Brian Paul

Directed by Lee MacDougall
Set and Costumes Designed by Michael Gianfrancesco
Lighting Designed by Robert Thomson
Stage Manager: Beth Bruck
Assistant Stage Manager: Erin Fitzgerald
Apprentice Stage Manager: Matthew MacInnis
Composer/Music Director: Charles T. Cozens
Publicity: John McHenry

Characters

Billy, a young, single worker
Nate, a Stelco worker
Rose, Nate's wife
Louis, a worker of Italian origin
Marie, Louis' girlfriend and later his wife
Alice, Reg's wife
Reg, a leader of Local 1005
Frank, brother of Reg
A Relief Officer
Tim Buck, Leader of the Labour-Progressive Party
Hugh Hilton, President of Stelco
Olive Kelly, Hilton's public relations assistant
Sam Lawrence, Mayor of Hamilton
Nora-Frances Henderson, Hamilton City Controller

Glory Days

The Play

ACT ONE

Overture.

The set suggests a steel mill with towers, ladders, large windows and hard angular metal pieces. Two twelve-foot-high towers are on the rear stage right and left making a second level. As the overture plays, the sky is aflame as if from the glow from a furnace or molten steel in a giant ladle. Figures are seen climbing over the set and then, as the music concludes, eight individuals are standing in spots. BILLY is in centre stage and the others flank him.

BILLY Maybe some of you here tonight know something about the Stelco strike of 1946. The "Glory Days" as some have called it. That strike was a victory, a milestone for the people of Hamilton – the people of Canada. It changed things for us all.

It changed me.

Now imagine this to be the whole of Stelco and the city of Hamilton where it was born. Imagine us to be not eight but the thousands and thousands of people involved. The fighters, the winners, the losers, the scabs, management, labour, politicians: all the men and women who were caught up in making the change.

So call me Billy. I grew up in the north end where workin' people stuck together to survive.

As each individual speaks their spot grows brighter.

NATE So call me Nate. I'm Polish born and Hamilton raised. So what do you want? Perfection?

ROSE Call me Rose. I was born and raised on a farm near Woodstock. I came to Hamilton when I was seventeen with my sister. She went home a year later, but by then I'd met Nate, and I wasn't going anywhere.

LOUIS Call me a Wop and I'll kill you! My name's Louis.

MARIE Call me Marie. I was raised a good Catholic girl. A husband, a baby and probably another baby. Life sure holds some surprises.

ALICE Call me Alice. Born in Scotland, 1911. God made me for a purpose.

REG Call me Reg. After our father died my big brother made sure I got a Grade 12 education. Hamilton Tech. Things were gonna be better for me. A union? I don't think I knew what that really meant.

FRANK Call me Frank. Reg is my little brother. I went to work when I was 15 and I worked hard all of my life. I like hard work. Hard work's good for the soul.

A projection reads "1938." Everyone exits except BILLY and NATE.

NATE Let's go, Billy!

BILLY Where're we goin'?

NATE What's wrong with you, dummy? You wanna get on relief, don't you?

BILLY Ya – but Nate – I'm just…

NATE Come on. Everyone's gotta do it.

BILLY I guess so.

They start walking.

NATE They piss me off. Know what? A relief officer come right into the house the other day. Rosie was there lookin' after the kids and they came in and they says, they says, *(mimicking)* "We have a complaint that Nate is drinkin' beer."

BILLY Were ya?

NATE Me? Drinkin' beer? *(laughs)* Looked under the bed for empty beer bottles, and everythin'. Jeeze, I ask you, can't a man even have a bottle of beer in this country?

ALICE and MARIE enter. They keep walking on their way to the Relief Office. ALICE is pregnant.

ALICE I was workin' as a seamer making relief underwear in Mercury Mills, there near Gage Park.

MARIE That's supposed to be a good place to work.

ALICE Soon as they found out I was having this *(points to her stomach)*, I was out the door.

MARIE They don't give a fig about you.

ALICE I tried to cover it up by stuffing my boobs so they'd think I'd put on the lard, but it didna do any good.

NATE touches his hat in greeting to the women.

NATE Alice, Marie, this is Billy. No work. He needs relief.

REG enters with LOUIS and FRANK.

REG Single men don't get relief, kid.

REG kisses ALICE. LOUIS tips his hat to MARIE. They keep moving on their way to the Relief Office.

FRANK Lotsa families in need.

NATE His mom is sick.

LOUIS Where's your Papa?

BILLY He left years ago.

MARIE You might get it.

ALICE Dunna hurt to try.

They have arrived at the Relief Office. The actors carry chairs onto the stage and set them up in a row. The RELIEF OFFICER, standing at her desk, looks suspiciously at the group.

BILLY *(to NATE)* How much do you get on relief anyway?

NATE Two dollars and twenty-five cents a week.

MARIE And to get that you gotta come to the Relief Office and line up all day.

They sit in the row of chairs. As the scene progresses, the actors move from chair to chair.

RELIEF OFFICER Next!

LOUIS Keep movin', Billy.

The actors all move down one chair towards the RELIEF OFFICER's desk.

BILLY There's a lot of chairs in here.

ROSE enters and joins the group beside NATE.

ROSE And you're gonna sit in every one of them.

RELIEF OFFICER Next!

A man in bad shoes approaches the RELIEF OFFICER's desk.

ALICE Up one row—

NATE And down the next.

He offers his chair to ROSE. She declines.

BILLY What do they want to know?

RELIEF OFFICER Name?

MARIE Treat you like you were a criminal.

RELIEF OFFICER Gender?

LOUIS Make you feel so small you squirm.

NATE To get a pair of shoes re-soled you have to show them to her.

RELIEF OFFICER *(examining the shoes worn by the man applying for relief)* Ah ha…

The relief worker examines the shoes of a welfare recipient in the 2006 production of *Glory Days* as the others look on.
l to r: Kate Henning, Brian Paul. *top row:* Tara Hughes, Paolo Mancini, Ryan Hollyman.
bottom row: George Masswohl, Tim Campbell, Caden Douglas,
Lina Giornofelice, Stephanie McNamara.
photo by Roy Timm

ROSE	And they have to be totally worn out.
ALICE	I'm sick of it all.
REG	Hey, Nate, you still doin' your government relief work?
NATE	Last week I was mixin' cement on the sweat boards at the Botanical Gardens, just about killed me.
ROSE	He just drags himself home like a dog. If we didn't have the kids, I'd say to hell with their relief.

The RELIEF OFFICER gives the man a chit for new shoes. He exits.

NATE	The worst was last summer, up on the Sherman Cut. That's how I got my fallen arches.
RELIEF OFFICER	Next!

FRANK moves up to the desk and talks earnestly with the RELIEF OFFICER.

ROSE He couldn't even take off his shoes and socks by himself, so guess who…?

NATE I finally saved enough money to go and see a doctor about them. He says…

ROSE *(mimicking the doctor)* "Go to the store and buy yourself a pair of arch supports."

NATE *(objecting humorously)* They cost fifteen cents.

ROSE I said: "There goes my honeymoon!" *(They laugh.)*

FRANK moves back to the group.

RELIEF OFFICER Next!

NATE and ROSE move up to the desk and talk to the RELIEF OFFICER. ALICE stands up, stretching her back.

ALICE I hate this waitin', making us line up like beggars.

BILLY Are you goin' to have a baby?

ALICE You noticed!

They all laugh at BILLY's naiveté.

REG We can't afford to have kids. I even rode the rails out to the West Coast and back. No work there either. Alice, she hadn't told her boss that we were married.

ALICE They woulda fired me on the spot.

BILLY They wouldn't do that, would they?

Again they all laugh at BILLY.

ALICE At the Mercury Mills we had to be in at seven in the morning and work till six at night for twenty-two cents an hour.

LOUIS Good money for a woman.

ALICE We had a union. That's what saved our skin.

REG But then they brought in the piecework system—

ALICE Aye—

REG And Alice—

ALICE *(She looks disapprovingly at REG.)* Whose story is it?

REG Oh. Sorry.

NATE and ROSE move back to the group.

MARIE I worked by the piece once – just about killed me.

ALICE Turned out the piece rates were even less than twenty-two cents an hour. So we struck! We were off for weeks walkin' on that picket line.

RELIEF OFFICER Next!

ALICE We won the strike though. End of the piece rate and twenty-five cents an hour.

RELIEF OFFICER *(annoyed to be kept waiting)* Next!

BILLY jumps up quickly and stands before the RELIEF OFFICER. They talk intently.

ROSE At least you've got your brother to help you out.

REG & ALICE Rock of Gibraltar.

FRANK Ya, well, we have to stick together or we'd starve.

REG Frank always comes through when we need him.

FRANK I was workin' in the light bulb factory over on York Street. Then even I got laid off.

ALICE Things are really tough with Frank out of work.

FRANK Believe me, you can't buy a job in this town.

The RELIEF OFFICER slams her ledger down on her desk in disgust.

RELIEF OFFICER What do you think this is? There is no relief for single men!

The people at the Relief Office disperse. The couples pair off and start to exit, carrying the chairs, leaving a despondent BILLY alone at the centre of the stage. REG looks back and sees him.

REG Don't worry, kid. We'll find you somethin'. *(BILLY nods.)* You got any family?

BILLY Nah. *(beat)* Just my mom. *(The others are gone.)* You?

REG Just Frank and Alice.

They start to walk.

BILLY Frank your brother?

REG Older. He's a bit of a jerk sometimes, but…

BILLY He's so serious.

REG Ya, he had to start workin' real young. But when we were kids, we used to goof around all the time.

BILLY Really?

REG We used to climb bridges. Frank was crazy.

FRANK appears high on the tower stage left, looking down. He is twelve years old. REG is eight. BILLY watches the scene.

FRANK Don't come up here, Reggie.

REG Why not?

FRANK This high is for big kids. Little kids aren't allowed.

REG Are too! *(REG starts to climb.)*

FRANK You're gonna fall! *(REG continues to climb.)* I'm not catchin' you. And I'm not catchin' it when you break your neck.

REG I won't.

FRANK That's high enough. *(He looks out.)* You can see everythin' from up here.

REG What things?

FRANK All kinds of stuff. Adult stuff.

REG I'm comin'.

FRANK Feels like you're flying.

REG climbs up to FRANK's level.

REG *(unnerved)* Whoa.

FRANK Don't let go of that strut. Stand like this. An' let go.

He opens his arms, and balances on the edge. REG stands shakily. He hangs on with one hand.

REG You're gonna get it, Frankie.

FRANK No I'm not.

REG Yes you are. I'm tellin'.

FRANK You can't tell. You're up here too.

REG Show me what you were doin'.

FRANK Wait for the wind to die down. Then stand like this, *(He opens his arms.)* then let go.

REG is inches away from the strut. He lifts one arm. FRANK grabs the back of REG's shirt collar.

I got you.

REG lets go of the strut. The boys fly together with their arms apart, feeling the wind and sharing the moment.

REG It does feel like flyin'!

FRANK I told you. *(FRANK shakes REG, to scare him, and they both laugh.)* Whoohoo! *(FRANK still holds on to REG's shirt.)* I got you.

ALICE and MARIE enter with CCF (Co-operative Commonwealth Federation) posters. They are adults. Everyone is back in 1938 again.

ALICE *(looking up at the men)* Can you see anything?

REG No. Just more people comin' for the meetin'. No parade yet.

ALICE Well, get down from there. You're not kids, you know.

MARIE Even though they act like it.

The men climb down and join the women. BILLY joins the group. ALICE has various CCF campaign materials that she distributes to REG and MARIE. She is clearly the political organizer of the CCF effort.

ALICE *(to MARIE)* Make sure everyone gets a leaflet.

BILLY Isn't this a Communist rally?

ALICE gives REG a big sign saying "Vote CCF." Another sign says "CCF supports Unions." Sounds offstage, a drum, singing.

SINGERS
No more tradition's charge shall bind us.
Arise, you slave no more in thrall.
The earth shall rise on new foundations.
We have been naught. We shall be all!

ALICE *(speaking over the singing)* Yes, but it's a great opportunity to tell people about the CCF. And they're always at our meetings. Now, dunna get pushed around by these Commies, Reg!

BILLY has climbed up to the second level. He points offstage excitedly.

BILLY Tim Buck is comin'!

MARIE *(a joke)* Tim Buck who? *(the others laugh)*

BILLY Tim Buck! The head of the Communist Party! Right here in Woodlands Park!

The parade enters, led by a woman pounding on a big drum. There are cheers. In the centre of the group is Tim BUCK, the leader of the Labour-Progressive Party, wearing a suit and tie. He shakes hands and waves. BILLY joins the Communist group singing a rousing chorus of "The Internationale."

MARCHERS
Arise, you prisoners of starvation.
Arise, you wretched of the earth.
For justice thunders condemnation,
For a better world's in birth.

BUCK climbs up on a soap box holding his arms out and beaming happily. The crowd gathers around to listen to his speech. The first few words are said over the hubbub of the crowd, but then people settle to listen.

BUCK Terrific! What a great Hamilton welcome! Thank you! Thank you! I am strengthened and encouraged by this enthusiastic response. But I'm here to tell you that this election is a great opportunity for working people. The owners of the steel companies live in splendour while the working people, who create the wealth, live in dire need. It is time for a radical change of the system!

NATE *(aside to BILLY)* All politics is crap.

BILLY *(to NATE)* No. Communism's for the poor people.

BUCK We must overthrow this system of injustice! Time for action! *WORKERS OF THE WORLD, UNITE*!

There are cheers and applause.

BILLY *(shouting over the others)* That's right!

NATE Bullshit!

BUCK *(continuing his speech)* I have to ask. Why are you people here?

FRANK 'Cause we're out of work!

BUCK And who put you out of work? The capitalist system!

A few cheers of agreement.

We've got to organize the working class.

BILLY How?

BUCK We've got to build the party and the unions! That's the road to power! Only the Labour-Progressive Party will change the system.

LOUIS *(to BILLY)* What's Labour Progressive?

BILLY *(to LOUIS)* The Communists!

LOUIS *(heckling BUCK)* What about me, eh? No job!

BUCK There'll be jobs for everyone! We'll own the steel companies, the banks. We'll end the Depression! A vote for the Labour-Progressive Party is a vote for the end of slave labour. Vote for progress, VOTE LABOUR-PROGRESSIVE!

There are more cheers as BUCK steps off the soap box. He works the crowd, shaking hands and chatting.

LOUIS *(to NATE and BILLY)* I deliver for grocery store. I don't get no pay.

BILLY That's exploitation! The Communists will do somethin' about that.

NATE Grow up, Billy. Politicians don't do nothin'.

BILLY Yer wrong! I'm gonna talk to Mr. Buck.

REG and ALICE have joined the group and have heard the last comments.

REG The Commies are too radical.

ALICE An' the Liberals an' Conservatives are too busy scratchin' each other's backsides. The CCF is the party for workers like us, the Co-operative Commonwealth Federation.

BILLY We need fighters. Not CCF stooges!

ALICE Have you heard Tommy Douglas speak? Or Sam Lawrence? Reasonable politicians who support the working man, that's what we need.This leaflet explains it all.

ALICE gives BILLY a leaflet and points to a passage on it.

REG See? We need co-ops to run things. And we need unions!

BILLY And the Communists will make it happen.

BILLY moves to meet Tim BUCK.

NATE Come on, Rose. I'm tired of this crap!

MARIE *(handing ROSE a pamphlet)* You should read this. Women have to get involved in politics.

NATE takes the pamphlet from ROSE. He crumples it up and throws it away as they exit. The drum is banged again. The Communist group sings a few lines of "The Internationale," as BUCK, BILLY and the others march out.

MARCHERS
Arise, you prisoners of starvation.
Arise, you wretched of the earth.

The song fades. The others gather up their things and exit, leaving MARIE and LOUIS alone on the stage. They are cleaning up flyers and streamers. They are coy and shy with each other.

MARIE That was real brave, speakin' up like that.

LOUIS No. It was nothin'.

MARIE You're Louis, aren't you?

LOUIS How you know that?

MARIE I know the store where you deliver. I'm Marie. They really don't pay you anythin'?

LOUIS I get a few tips. And the grocer, he cut a dollar off the family food bill. Poppa say everythin' helps.

MARIE Must be hard.

LOUIS *(He stands up straight, as if to show how strong he is.)* I look after myself. Look for a real job.

MARIE Where's your dad workin'?

LOUIS Stelco.

MARIE Mine too.

LOUIS They call it Wop City down there.

MARIE I don't like that word, Louis. You're no Wop.

LOUIS I know! I not even Italian. I'm Sicilian!

MARIE Really?

LOUIS We have to shop at Italian stores. No one else give us credit.

MARIE My family runs a tab at the store you work for.

LOUIS That's where I see you.

MARIE I was probably askin' for more credit – to buy stockings or somethin'.

LOUIS Ya, about six guys give you the eye.

MARIE *(coyly)* Ah, go on.

LOUIS But I say to them, I say, hey! You better watch out. She's a good Italian girl.

MARIE You said that?

LOUIS I told 'em I gotta claim on you, jus' to scare 'em off.

MARIE Really?

Beat.

LOUIS Hey, there's a dance at the Winter Garden Saturday night. You come with me?

MARIE smiles. Suddenly NATE comes running in.

NATE *(shouting)* Louis! Louis! Stelco's hirin' for the make up gang! Seven o'clock, Wilcox Gate!

MARIE runs off.

The wire mesh gate has been slid into place, making a barrier between the men and the plant. LOUIS, NATE, BILLY, FRANK, REG and other men are shaking the gate and fence. A FOREMAN is up on the second level. There are shouts and even some shoving as the desperate men attempt to get the attention of the FOREMAN. The comments pile on top of each other. The action is chaotic.

BILLY Me! Me!

LOUIS I work hard!

NATE Come on! Gimme a chance!

REG Choose me! Me!

FRANK I'm yer man!

FOREMAN *(pointing at FRANK)* You.

FRANK enters through the plant gates and disappears, as the others continue to shout to get attention.

LOUIS Me! I need a job!

FOREMAN You.

Another worker enters through the gate.

NATE I need work! Me!

FOREMAN You.

Another worker enters through the gate.

BILLY Me! Please!

FOREMAN That's all for today.

The gate is closed. The FOREMAN exits and BILLY, NATE, REG and LOUIS turn away dejectedly as they exit. The lights change and the sounds of the mill rise to a roar. The gates roll open to show the inside of the mill where FRANK is shovelling slag. LOUIS enters, carrying a shovel.

LOUIS Frank – good to see you!

FRANK Hey, Louis.

LOUIS My poppa, he spoke to his boss. Got me hired on.

FRANK Better get workin'. Foreman's watchin'.

As the two men shovel, they sing. The sound of the mill changes to become the music accompanying the singing; it still has an industrial sound.

MEN

We sing the song of the molten ore,
Of steel which boils as the white flames roar;
Our furnaces set the sky a-glow
Men toil and sweat in the heat below.

REG enters carrying a large broom.

REG Can't thank you enough, Frankie. First time I've had a real job in… in years.

FRANK Told them you were a good worker. Don't let me down.

NATE comes in with a big shovel.

NATE Reg! Louis! *(NATE shakes their hands enthusiastically.)* Turns out my next door neighbour is a crew chief. Good to see you guys.

FRANK Get workin' or you'll be out the door before your first paycheque.

REG, LOUIS and NATE sing as they work with the others.

MEN

We tell of mills, which press and squeeze,
And shears, which cut the bars like cheese.
The furnaces blast like a breath from hell.
There's a constant roar from the finishing mills.

BILLY comes running in, carrying a big broom.

BILLY Nate, how did you get me on?!

NATE We take care of each other.

REG *(teasing)* Just like a good Commie, eh Nate?

The men laugh, and start to work again. As they work, all the men sing with musical accompaniment.

MEN

We're Stelco men, you've heard of our fame.
Steelworkin' men, and proud of our name.

The men take a quick rest, glancing around anxiously to make sure the FOREMAN does not see them.

REG I need a break.

NATE Foreman's gone for a smoke, but he's a sneaky son-of-a-bitch.

BILLY Doesn't this place ever shut down?

The men laugh.

FRANK A steel mill's a twenty-four-hour-a-day operation.

LOUIS Seven days a week.

NATE Yesterday, on the open hearth there was a break out. Slag poured out all over the floor. Melted the rubber right off the bottom of my boots.

REG Musta' been 150 degrees.

LOUIS Summer – you die from the heat in this place. I can' take it much longer.

FRANK Got to look after yourself, Louis. Wear your sweatbands and sweat caps.

NATE And heavy jeans and woollen underwear. You gotta do that or your dick'll burn off.

BILLY You think this is bad? They shifted Louis and me over to the sheet mill for a few days.

BILLY and LOUIS are carrying something heavy.

LOUIS Had to wrestle with the steel. Pull it out and push it back.

BILLY Some of it musta' weighed six hundred pounds!

All of the men sing.

MEN

Steel that cuts and burns our hands.
In heat that's more than a guy can stand,
We work like slaves as hard as we can,
It's steel can break the soul of a man.

REG watches the men work, then moves toward his home. A small kitchen rolls out onto stage left. ALICE is cooking. In the background the men continue to work.

ALICE Hello, handsome. You're home awfully early. Dinner's not quite ready yet. It's bubblin' sweet.

She gives REG a kiss but he says nothing. She chatters on while REG sits, dejected.

I was at the doctor's today. He said the baby is going to be big and healthy. Oh, and I was over to Frankie's to borrow some baby clothes from that crabby Myrtle. An' I think I'd like to get some wallpaper for the baby's room, but 'tis awful dear. So I was thinkin' maybe we can paint it some unusual colours. What do you think of that, Reggie?

REG *(preoccupied)* Ummmm…

ALICE Ach, I do go on, dun I? How was your day?

REG There was another accident today. Sam Beagle.

ALICE What happened?

REG They were dumpin' a truckload of slag. Sam's been workin' fifteen hours a day for the past three weeks. Anyway, a huge piece bounced off the truck and landed on his foot.

ALICE Ach, no!

REG Smashed it up real bad. When I got there, the foreman says: "Tell the men it was his own fault." I blew my top, Alice. I told the bastard that if he didn't work the men so hard they'd be able to react quicker. It isn't safe!

ALICE What did he say to that?

REG Never said a word, but when we got back from takin' Sam to the hospital the superintendent told me that I was on the string. He said that he'd call when they needed me, and that the next step for a shit disturber is out the kick!

ALICE You did the right thing, Reg.

REG Alice, I'm laid off. We have no money.

ALICE Jus' never you mind your wee head about that, dearie. We'll manage.

REG Maybe if I go and apologize to the foreman. Tell him I was wrong.

ALICE But you weren't!

REG But it would get me off the string.

REG rises, and moves back toward the other men, as they sing the chorus.

MEN We're Stelco men, you've heard of our fame.
Steelworkin' men, and proud of our name.

The men are dressing BILLY in a heavy jacket and gloves.

BILLY What are the checkers, anyway?

LOUIS The firebricks that line the furnace get corroded and fall in.

REG You've gotta go in and pull out the old bricks, Billy.

FRANK Youngest guy in the bull gang gets the job.

NATE They've cooled the furnace down for about eight hours.

LOUIS But it still gonna be hot. Two hundred degrees!

The noise from the blast furnace rises to a crescendo. The men shout to be heard.

FRANK Put the scarf around his head!

They cover his head with a hat, and his face with a scarf.

REG Throw out the bricks as fast as you can, and then get out!

NATE And watch your dick! It's so hot in there it could burn off.

BILLY is handed tongs by NATE. Red heat glows out of the furnace door. BILLY stands for a moment in front of the door, his body silhouetted. The intensity of the sound increases. The men get more and more frantic, their voices reflecting the panic.

REG Don't wait to get a suntan, Billy!

LOUIS Hurry, Billy! Hurry!

FRANK Faster, Billy!

BILLY drops the tongs and then collapses to the floor.

Billy prepares to go into a furnace to clear the fallen fire bricks, called "checkers."
This was one of the most dangerous jobs in the plant.
l to r: Ryan Hollyman, Caden Douglas, Tim Campbell.
photo by Roy Timm

NATE Shit! Get outta there!

FRANK He's down!

LOUIS *(screaming)* Billy!

LOUIS is close to the mouth of the furnace and is thrown back with the heat. REG goes to help LOUIS. NATE goes into the furnace and hauls BILLY back by his legs. The action is frantic.

NATE Get him some water!

LOUIS Billy, you okay?!

They unwrap his head to give him air. BILLY is not moving.

REG Come on, Billy! Come on! Come on!

BILLY *(BILLY stirs and coughs.)* Oh, shit. My head!

The men lift him to sitting. The volume of the sound lowers.

An excited MARIE calls LOUIS. The men resume working. LOUIS rushes over.

MARIE Louis!

LOUIS What?

MARIE What took you so long?

LOUIS I'm comin', Maria.

LOUIS runs into MARIE's arms. Then she spins around to show him her new outfit.

LOUIS Oh hey. You look so pretty.

MARIE I'm all ready. Go home and get dressed. We're supposed to be there in a half an hour.

LOUIS You make that dress?

MARIE Well, Mamma helped a little, but I did most of it.

LOUIS It's beautiful.

MARIE Oh, Louis. I can't believe there'll be a three-piece orchestra for the reception.

LOUIS Look, Marie. I'm sorry, but… I can' go to the wedding.

MARIE What?

LOUIS The foreman, he say I work overtime tonight. Re-brick the furnace.

MARIE But Louis, it's Gina's wedding.

LOUIS I'm sorry.

MARIE Ohhhh. Wednesday night you couldn't make the movie.

LOUIS I know.

MARIE Then Sunday night you couldn't make it to dinner.

LOUIS Sorry.

MARIE My folks are startin' to wonder, Louis.

LOUIS Well…

MARIE Well – never mind. I'll dance with Vinny.

LOUIS *(panicked)* Vinny! I can' do nothin' about it, Marie!

MARIE Why not?!

LOUIS 'Cause I'm low man on the crew.

MARIE Well then, maybe you shouldn't be down there.

LOUIS I gotta work!

MARIE They treat you like a slave!

LOUIS Look! You wanna get married?

MARIE Ya.

LOUIS You wanna have family?

MARIE Ya.

LOUIS You wanna buy a house beside your mamma?

MARIE *(She smiles and nods.)* Ya!

LOUIS Then shut up!

As LOUIS rejoins the other men in the plant, MARIE runs off, and the men work and sing the final chorus of the "Stelco Song."

MEN

We're Stelco men, you've heard of our pain.
Steelworkin' men, and damned all the same.

LOUIS has climbed up the scaffolding. He slips and is hanging by one arm. LOUIS screams.

LOUIS *Helllllp*!!!

The men come rushing to help him. There is a confusion of shouts.

REG Hang on, Louis!

BILLY I've got you!

NATE Hold on!

FRANK Now let go!

LOUIS is pulled to safety by the others.

LOUIS I tell that son-of-a-bitch foreman! "There's oil all over that walkway," an' you know what he say? He say, "You don' like workin' here, then get outta the plant. A thousand more Dagos standin' outside the gate."

REG Come on, Louis, I'll buy you at beer at Nelligan's.

BILLY Hey, that was a pretty good trick.

NATE Ya, your people work in the circus?

The men laugh as they move into Joey Nelligan's speakeasy. It is relaxed. Glen Miller type music plays in the background. They settle onto chairs and boxes to talk.

I'll get the first round. Got to get the taste of that plant out of my throat.

NATE grabs five beers from a case and passes them around.

BILLY Hey, Reg, do you know Borkovitch?

REG You mean Ivan the Terrible?

BILLY Ya, ya – him. Well, when they put me in the bar mill, he got bumped back to the bull gang, and I was forced to take his job.

REG Nice guy!

NATE I didn't think a good Commie would do a thing like that.

BILLY Hey, I didn't want to do it. I told the foreman I didn't think it was fair, and he said either I get on the job or get the hell out of the plant.

FRANK What else could you do?

LOUIS Foreman always give the good jobs to the Anglos.

REG You know Miller, the foreman in the rolling mill? On payday he hangs his coat in the change house and all the men in his crew have to put money in his pocket.

NATE The bastard!

FRANK Why don't you guys quit beefin'? It ain't gonna change.

REG Sometimes I think you don't want it to change.

FRANK says nothing.

BILLY Bobby Bilko was sick for a week last month. I heard he was so afraid of losin' his job that he took his crew boss home, put a bottle of whiskey on the table and left him with his wife for a couple of hours.

NATE That's nothin'. I had this one asshole foreman who gave me a couple of ducks he shot. Told me I had to pluck them for him. So he came back about a half an hour later and I'm sittin' there with this duck on my lap and he says, "What the hell are you doin'? I told you to pluck that duck." I said "Oh, *(beat)* pluck?"

All the men laugh.

REG Ah, you're always braggin', aren't ya?

NATE You too, eh Reggie, now that you've got Alice.

REG *(laughing)* Get off it.

NATE *(mimicking ALICE's accent)* Ach, Reggie. Do you follow the wee woman?

They all laugh, even REG.

REG I'll tell ya, I'm fed up with that whole stinkin' mess. Somethin's gotta change.

FRANK You're always tryin' to buck the system.

REG Well, I sure as hell am not gonna pay any foreman for a job.

NATE *(sarcastically)* You wouldn't do that, would you, Frankie?

FRANK I might if it meant gettin' off the bull gang.

BILLY You wouldn't.

FRANK You guys just don't know how that place works. *(to REG)* And you, you don't have the right to be so damned high and mighty. How do you think you got off the string? A personal commendation from the boss?

Beat.

REG *(shocked) You* got me back? You paid my way back in? *(FRANK says nothing.)* Oh shit! Shit!

REG gets up, grabs his jacket, and walks out of the speakeasy. The other men continue talking at Joey Nelligan's. REG and ALICE's kitchen slides out. ALICE is cooking.

(angry and frustrated) It makes me feel sick!

ALICE It's not your fault, Reg.

REG Here I thought I got off the string because I was keepin' my mouth shut, but really it was because Frank paid off the foreman. It's never gonna change, Alice.

ALICE Well, there's no point sulking at home. Somebody's got to start the ball rolling.

REG You think it's so easy…

ALICE No I don't! But I'm a Glaswegian. Grew up on the Red Clyde, where they fight for workers. The same stuff was going on in Mercury Mills. We changed things by getting a union.

REG If I even mention that word I'll be out on my ass.

ALICE There've been unions at Stelco. Those men weren't afraid of risk.

REG Those were the skilled men. Not labourers like me.

ALICE What about the workers in the sheet mill? They've got the Independent Steelworkers Union.

REG The company has never recognized them.

ALICE Look, Reg, all I'm saying is that a lot of the workers down there must think the same way you do, but they dunna know what to do about it. They need leadership – someone to follow, Reggie. Talk to them.

REG I'm not the guy!

ALICE Then get someone from outside the plant to talk to them. A labour man like Sam Lawrence would…

REG You don't know what it's like down there. If it got out that I was organizing…

ALICE The way I see it, you've got two choices. You can either be like your ox-headed brother, and put up with it, or you can change it. As my old Granny used to say:

TOGETHER "Shit or get off the pot!" *(They laugh together.)*

There is laughter from the men at Joey Nelligan's. They put the boxes and chairs away.

BILLY Hey, Louis, it all comes down from on high, you know. It all comes from Hilton.

LOUIS How you know?

Hugh HILTON, Stelco's President, enters and pauses, surveying the mill.

BILLY Mr. Hugh Hilton: capitalist pig. He sets the standards and the foremen follow 'em.

LOUIS That Commie talk, Billy.

BILLY How do you think he got to be Stelco president?

NATE You see the office staff? Rushin' down there every mornin'? Tryin' to get there before him?

Everyone lines up on the stairs. Hugh HILTON walks up the stairs past them.

MAVIS Mr. Hilton.

MARIE Good day, Mr. Hilton.

ALICE Mornin', Mr. Hilton.

NATE Steel's sellin', Mr. Hilton.

ROSE Nice to see you, Mr. Hilton.

LOUIS Hope the company doin' well, Mr. Hilton.

REG May I take your hat, Mr. Hilton?

BILLY May I shine your boots, Mr. Hilton?

NATE Like a pack a' hungry dogs, barkin' for their master.

All but REG and BILLY exit. HILTON sits at his desk. REG knocks at the door to HILTON's office, which is up on the second level.

HILTON Come in.

REG and BILLY enter HILTON's office. REG has his cap in his hand. BILLY puts on a brave front but even he is intimidated to be in the presence of the great man of Stelco.

REG Mr. Hilton. We're from Work Gang number four.

HILTON What're your names?

REG I'm Reg Gibson, sir, and… and this is Billy Brett.

He writes down their names.

HILTON Yes?

REG Well, sir, it's like this. We think that the foreman of the bull gang doesn't treat the men very well, and… and we think that you maybe could do somethin' about it, sir.

HILTON You think you deserve to be treated better?

BILLY Well, yes, sir.

HILTON He's too tough on you, is he?

BILLY On all the men, sir.

REG It's the unfairness, sir.

HILTON stands up and delivers his message in a forthright, authoritarian manner.

HILTON The job of my foremen is to make sure the employees work hard for this company. It's not easy. I run a steel mill, not a girl's school. Get this straight! I built this company. I redesigned this plant from top to bottom and finally got it running profitably. Do you think I'm going to lose it all to a bunch of complainers and whiners?

REG No sir, but…

HILTON There's trouble overseas that might lead to a war. If there is a war, this plant will be very important to the Allied effort. I won't have men coming in here with sob stories about their foreman, and I won't have a union in here telling me what to do. It's tough in this mill, and I expect the men who work here to be as tough as the steel they are producing. Do you understand?

Beat.

Now, I've got work to do. Good day, gentlemen.

Humiliated, REG and BILLY exit. HILTON stays at his desk, writing.

NATE and ROSE's sitting room rolls out on stage right. NATE enters and crosses to his home where ROSE waits for him.

NATE Hey, Rosie, I'm home.

ROSE We missed you tonight.

NATE No, I'm not hungry. I ate.

ROSE I wasn't talking about supper.

NATE Well, what then?

ROSE His birthday.

NATE Whose?

ROSE Bobby's.

NATE *(suddenly realizing)* Oh no! I'll go up and see him.

ROSE No, leave him alone. He just fell asleep. Where were you?

NATE Nelligan's. Just for one.

ROSE That's every night this week.

NATE Well, you try and work a ten-hour shift in that stink hole. I need a drink to wind down.

ROSE Why can't you drink at home?

NATE 'Cause Nelligan's is a good place to let off steam. You want me to do that here?

ROSE Ya, ya, I want that. Look, I hardly ever see you, and the kids never see you.

NATE I see them on my day off.

ROSE No you don't. You sleep all day.

NATE turns away from her.

We need you, Nate.

NATE turns back and pleads with her.

NATE It'll get better, Rosie. I'm gonna get switched to the bar mill. It'll be way better. You'll see.

ROSE When's that gonna be?

NATE Listen, Reg and Alice are havin' a party tomorrow night. An' the wives are invited.

ROSE Another party?

NATE Can you get a babysitter?

Beat.

ROSE Let's go to bed.

ALICE and REG's kitchen slides into place. The party has begun. Big Band music is playing. NATE and ROSE are slow-dancing. LOUIS and MARIE join them on the dance floor. ALICE and FRANK talk. REG is serving drinks. BILLY is very drunk. He climbs up onto a kitchen chair, holding a newspaper, and speaks in a loud voice.

BILLY Listen.... Listen to this. *(reading)* "Tension is still high in the capitals of Europe today as the world awaits further details from London and Berlin.

On the national scene, Steelworker President, John L. Lewis, today announced that the C.I.O. is determined to bring onion... unionization to the steel industry of Canada."

They laugh at BILLY.

NATE Onionization?

REG *(making a speech)* All right. Okay. Before everyone gets completely blotto, let me remind you why we're celebratin'. I propose a toast. *(holds up his glass)* To the establishment of our own Stelco local of the United Steelworkers Union, Local...

They all hold their glasses high.

EVERYONE LOCAL 1005!

Cheers and congratulations.

MARIE Enough of the speeches. It's supposed to be a party.

REG All right. But seriously, seriously. We've got to get out and sign people up for the union.

BILLY Let's sign 'em all up!

NATE *(laughing)* Billy, Hilton calls himself a steelworker. Why don't you go and sign him up?

BILLY Hilton's a fascist. The companies put their jackboots on when they talk to unions. We have to organize the working class.

BILLY hugs NATE drunkenly.

ROSE Nate, come and dance with me.

BILLY No one can stop the power of the working class!

FRANK That's right, Billy. Workers of the world unite. You have nothin' to lose but your jobs.

A toast to Local 1005.
l to r: Caden Douglas, Ryan Hollyman, Stephanie McNamara, Lina Giornofelice, Paolo Mancini, George Masswohl, Tim Campbell, Tara Hughes.
photo by Roy Timm

The three couples are dancing.

NATE You tell 'im, Frank.

BILLY *(singing drunkenly)* Arise, you sisters of starvation…

BILLY is interrupted by an angry LOUIS.

LOUIS Hey Billy, tha's enough!

BILLY *(ignoring LOUIS)* Arise, you wretched of the earth.

MARIE Leave him alone.

LOUIS *(to MARIE)* Too much of his bullshit.

MARIE pulls LOUIS away and they resume dancing. ALICE tries to distract BILLY.

ALICE Comrade, how are you?

BILLY Comrade Alice. This is a great meeting.

ALICE How's your mother doing?

BILLY Oh, she's real sick again.

ALICE I'm sorry to hear that.

BILLY Ya, it's not good. But hey, Alice. How do you tell a good Commie student from a bad Commie student?

ALICE I don't know.

BILLY By his Marx. *(BILLY laughs at his own joke.)* Get it? Karl Marx.

ALICE You better be careful. All this talk about the Communist Party's makin' some of the men nervous.

BILLY The Party will protect us.

ALICE Billy, we want them to join the union, not the Communist Party.

BILLY It's the same thing.

ALICE No, it's not the same thing.

BILLY drunkenly begins to sing again.

BILLY Arise, you sisters of starvation…

LOUIS confronts him.

LOUIS Billy!

REG intercepts him.

REG No, no, no, don't get into it.

LOUIS He piss me off, Reg.

NATE Go and have a drink, Louis.

REG You guys signed anyone up yet?

LOUIS I been talkin' to some a' the Italian guys. I get caught, I'm out on my ass.

NATE I've been puttin' the stickers up everywhere.

ROSE Oh, Nate. Not again.

NATE Just let me, Rosie. So I had all these stickers, right, that said "Join the Union," "Support Local 1005." Crap like that. An' one day I was stickin' 'em on the furnaces an' the boilers, when I was told to get my ass over to the main office, an' the boss he said to me…

ROSE *(plays the role of the superintendent in a mocking way)* "What the hell you think you're doin' puttin' Commie stickers all over the place?"

NATE "What stickers?"

ROSE "You know what stickers."

NATE is frustrated that she is making fun of his story.

NATE Rosie!

ROSE laughs.

(to REG) What sort of place is it that you get fired for stickin' stickers?

ROSE Oh come on!

ROSE pulls him towards her, and they begin to dance.

REG What about you, Frank? Are you gonna help out?

FRANK I dunno. I think we should give the Works Council a chance.

REG The Works Council are company stooges.

FRANK They got us new drinking fountains, didn't they?

REG What do the men want, a drinking fountain, or steady jobs?

FRANK Look, if we push the company too hard we could lose everythin'.

NATE What's a matter, Frankie? You afraid of old Hughie Hilton?

FRANK You're dammed right.

NATE Then you should get yourself a job as a foreman, and to hell with the rest of us.

(sings) The working class can kiss my ass,

The other men, except FRANK, join him good humouredly.

MEN I've got the foreman's job at last!
We'll rob the rich and rape the poor,
And make each working girl a…

They drop the word for the ladies' sake.

And did you really, really think
That we could have a…

ALICE has been listening to the radio intently.

ALICE *(waving at the others)* Quiet! Quiet!

REG What?

ALICE turns up the radio.

CHML "Prime Minister Mackenzie King is expected to recall Parliament immediately to deal with the emergency."

REG What is it?

ALICE We're going to war!

The party is over. ALICE turns off the radio. They all grab their things and exit. Parade marching music begins.

LOUIS runs to MARIE.

LOUIS Marie! Marie! They fired Dominic and Roscoe.

MARIE What?

LOUIS I go to the plant, same as always, but the guards, they don' let them in.

MARIE Why not?

LOUIS They members a' the Italian Club. Police say they all fascists.

MARIE Gino is the secretary there. Come on!

They run off. Parade music continues. NATE runs in carrying his kit bag and parts of his uniform. He drops his kit bag and begins putting on his army jacket and cap of his uniform.

NATE *(calling excitedly)* Rose! Rosie!

ROSE enters.

ROSE What is it?

NATE I gotta talk to you.

ROSE What are you doin'?

She is shocked to see him in a uniform.

NATE I signed up. I'm gonna get a ticket overseas.

ROSE You what?

NATE I joined up. *(sing-song voice)* I'm in the army now.

ROSE You're jokin'..

NATE No! Every time I turn on the radio I feel like a coward stuck at home. We can't let that crazy Kraut run all over us.

ROSE But how are we going to survive?

NATE I'll send you all my pay.

ROSE I thought they needed you in the plant!

NATE To hell with the plant. There's plenty in there, and anyway, I'll be back in six months. Don't worry, Rosie. If Hilton can't kill me, nobody can.

Beat. They look at each other. ROSE and NATE hug. NATE shoulders his kit bag, turns, and begins marching on the spot. ROSE fades back. LOUIS comes in wearing his army uniform. MARIE is on his arm.

MARIE You look so handsome.

LOUIS Maybe now they see I'm a Canadian, just like everyone else.

MARIE I was thinkin', Louis.

LOUIS Ya?

MARIE I was thinkin'. Can we get married before you go?

LOUIS What if I don' come back?

MARIE I want to be your wife!

LOUIS What about my family? My mother want a big wedding. And your mamma – she kill us!

MARIE Well, I'd die married!

LOUIS Anyway, I gotta ask *you*. You don' ask me.

MARIE Well ask me!

LOUIS You wanna?

MARIE Ya!

LOUIS Okay! I gotta go! Write me! Mi' Bella!

They kiss and hug. LOUIS joins NATE marching on the spot. MARIE waves and fades back. REG, FRANK and ALICE enter. REG is trying on an air force uniform and FRANK awkwardly tries on an army greatcoat.

REG But my country needs me, Alice!

ALICE What about your family?

REG You'll take care of them. I have to go where I'm needed more.

ALICE They need you here in the steel plant.

FRANK A war machine is built out of steel.

ALICE *(to FRANK)* And what about *your* family? Leaving Myrtle and the kids alone? You canna just run off in some adventure.

REG Adventure? Men are being killed overseas!

ALICE You'll contribute far more to the war effort by working in that steel mill than by throwing your life away somewhere.

FRANK *(fiddling with REG's jacket)* That thing doesn't even fit.

REG What about my duty to Canada?

ALICE You can get a deferment. You told me that workin' in the mill, making steel for the war effort, qualifies you for a deferment. Your duty is to stay right here in Hamilton and make steel!

REG and FRANK stop dressing. They both look at ALICE. Then they look at each other. They nod, and begin to take off the uniforms. The men start to fade back. BILLY enters in a naval uniform.

Billy.

BILLY Oh, hi Alice.

ALICE I heard that your mother died. I'm so sorry.

BILLY She was awful sick. The pain. It was a blessing.

ALICE What're you going to do now?

BILLY I'm all alone, so… so I've joined the navy.

ALICE A Communist in the King's navy? Won't be easy.

BILLY The party says we've got to fight fascism. I'm gonna be in the thick of it.

BILLY joins NATE and LOUIS marching. They all carry kit bags. The others exit. The marching men do a sharp left turn and march off. The parade music fades, and is replaced with the sound of bombs wailing and exploding. This fades as well.

MARIE and ROSE enter. MARIE is dressed in heavy work clothes. ROSE has her hair done up in a kerchief and wears a housedress.

ROSE You're workin' at Stelco?

MARIE Two months now. Since the men left, they need the bodies.

ROSE Does Louis know?

MARIE I wrote him about it, but he doesn't like it.

ROSE How is it?

MARIE Well it's rough. I'm on the railroad gang, fixin' track.

ROSE Must be hard work.

MARIE Gotta take care of ourselves. But you know Louis was right, the Stelco foremen are the worst.

ROSE Ya?

MARIE But the money's not bad. I could get you on if you want, Rose.

ROSE No, I got some house-cleaning jobs. That and lookin' after the boys is all I can handle.

MARIE Is Nate sendin' money home?

ROSE Ya, well, sometimes, but I've got steady customers and it puts food on the table. You know, one of my ladies is Mrs. Hilton.

MARIE No!

ROSE Ya, the wife of the big chief muckety-muck.

MARIE Bet she's got some secrets. *(laughs)*

ROSE Don't know about that, but she sure expects me to work. They all do. I thought this was supposed to last six months. All I ever do, work, work, work.

The women exit. REG and ALICE are at home.

REG These twelve-hour days are killers.

ALICE Westinghouse is just as bad.

FRANK enters.

FRANK Ready to go?

REG That mill is gonna be the death of me.

ALICE You wouldn'a have to work so long if you had a union.

FRANK Not that union crap again.

ALICE *(to FRANK)* You should be standing up to management.

REG The Steelworkers are growin'.

FRANK Ya, they'll be growing right out the door.

ALICE Did I tell you about the union the company started for us at Westinghouse, Frank?

FRANK Spare me.

ALICE The management tried to start a company union, an' guess what the workers called it? The Suckhole Society. An' what d'you think our real union told them they could do with their suck-hole society? I was right there when it happened. Told them they could stuff it where the sun don't shine.

REG and ALICE laugh while FRANK glowers.

REG That's somethin', eh Frankie?

FRANK If we ever tried that down at Stelco, Hilton'd have us out on the street before you could say "all in favour."

REG We're gonna stand up to him, Frank.

FRANK Ya, like your guys are standin' up behind the furnaces to collect dues.

REG At least we got the 1005 certified.

FRANK It didn't do you a damned bit of good. Hilton will never recognize any union.

REG Then I guess we'll just have to wait for the boys to come home.

Lights cross fade. They exit. HILTON sits at the desk in his office, while KELLY, a businesswoman in a practical woman's suit, stands near the door.

HILTON But I already *have* a secretary.

KELLY That's not why I'm here.

HILTON How did you get in?

KELLY I was sent to help you.

HILTON How could a woman help me?

KELLY I've worked with many companies like this one. I have excellent references.

She approaches his desk with letters in her hand.

HILTON I don't need any other staff.

KELLY Mr. Hilton, you need help listening, and with your communication skills…

HILTON I'll communicate this very clearly: *(yelling)* GET OUT!

KELLY That is clear, and it clearly shows the problem. We'll start there.

HILTON Start what? Who are you?

KELLY You can call me Miss Kelly.

HILTON Look, Miss Kelly…

KELLY Or you can call me Olive and I'll call you "Hugh."

HILTON I'm going to call security.

Picking up the telephone.

KELLY I wouldn't do that. I was sent here by the company's Board of Directors. Do you want it to get back to them that ol' Hughie Hilton couldn't deal with a woman?

HILTON puts the phone down.

HILTON The Board sent you?

KELLY To help you with P.R.

HILTON What's P.R.?

KELLY *(enunciating clearly)* Public Relations. You've been getting a lot of bad press lately.

Beat.

HILTON All right, Miss Kelly, let's have an understanding. I expect everyone to deal with me straight from the shoulder.

KELLY You mean "no bullshit?"

HILTON *(surprised by her nerve)* Well… yes. No bullshit.

Lights cross fade. A sign reads "Hamilton Station." A train is heard, and steam from a train blows out onto the stage. NATE, LOUIS and BILLY enter in their uniforms, singing. They are older, and a little battle-worn from being away so long.

NATE, BILLY & LOUIS

Oh you can't blame us
For fightin' with the Allies,

Fightin' with the Allies,
Fightin' with the Allies.

Oh you can't blame us
For fightin' with the Allies,
For fightin' with the Allies,
And winnin' that ol' war.

They stop, and look around. No one is there to meet them.

NATE Where is everybody?

LOUIS I thought my whole family be here.

BILLY I was supposed to get here yesterday.

NATE Maybe they came and left.

BILLY I bin waitin' months to be decommed.

LOUIS Now we wait again.

NATE *(seeing LOUIS' medals)* Ya got some hardware, eh Louis?

LOUIS Ya, Dieppe. *(beat)* Some never got off the beach. I got hit in the leg and my buddy, he grab holda' me and run. I got a medal for that wound, and he get nothin'.

NATE More than I got. I went over with Hamilton Light Infantry, expectin' action, but they gave me a motorcycle and dispatch duty.

BILLY A motorcycle!

NATE Ya, I was zippin' all over France and Holland, with officers shoutin' at me like I was low man in the bull gang.

LOUIS Ya, I know what you mean.

NATE But I gotta say the beer was pretty good.

LOUIS and BILLY nod and laugh.

BILLY I was North Atlantic, three years. When we made port in Halifax or Liverpool, I had a girl in every town.

NATE Horndog!

NATE and LOUIS laugh. On the second level, a WOMAN appears in silhouette.

WOMAN Billy! Billy!

BILLY They sure do like the boys in blue.

Other women call from off stage. The men are lost in their war memories.

FEMALE VOICES Billy! Billy! Billy!

The WOMAN exits. ALICE appears with REG and FRANK.

ALICE Billy!

BILLY turns to see ALICE, she runs to him and they hug. ROSE and MARIE enter from the other side.

ROSE Nate! You ol' bugger!

MARIE Louis!

ROSE and MARIE rush in and greet them. MARIE and LOUIS hug and kiss in an exuberant way. NATE spins ROSE in the air. ALICE fusses over BILLY. REG shakes his hand.

ALICE We were here all morning.

BILLY Good to see you, Alice.

REG Your old jobs at Stelco are waitin' for you.

MARIE Ya, they gave all us women the boot as soon as they could.

FRANK There's lots of work now.

LOUIS Anythin' change down there?

ALICE Not really.

MARIE Not a bit.

REG We got the union certified, but when it came time to join, only a few hundred signed up. They're still afraid of Hilton.

NATE Well I've been kicked around by Hitler, kicked around by officers, an' I'll be damned if I'm gonna be kicked around by that ol' son of a— *(ROSE stops his mouth with her hand.)*

LOUIS I did five years' service for this country. Nobody gonna call me Wop no more.

BILLY *(waving his fists)* I'm just hurtin' for it, know what I mean? Things have gotta change!

FRANK exits while the others sing.

MEN

Oh, you can't blame us
We're workin' for the union,
We're workin' for the union,
We're workin' for the union.

MEN & WOMEN

Oh, you can't blame us
We're workin' for the union,
We're workin' for the union.
All day and night.

As the song finishes, REG, NATE, LOUIS and BILLY climb the stairs to HILTON's office. They enter without knocking. HILTON is alone, seated at his desk.

REG Mr. Hilton.

HILTON Yes?

REG Mr. Hilton, we have been waiting for months now. We want to know why you won't negotiate a contract with us.

HILTON These things take time.

LOUIS You're stallin'!

REG The men are not goin' to be put off like this any longer.

NATE Sit down with us or we strike!

HILTON All four of you?

BILLY Why are we wastin' our time, Reg?

REG I don't think you realize how strong we've grown.

HILTON You have only five hundred men signed up. Why should I negotiate with you?

REG Every man in that plant will be allowed to vote, whether he's signed up or not.

LOUIS And they go out on strike, every man.

BILLY So if you're smart, you'll sit down and discuss our *(shouting)* very reasonable demands, right now!

HILTON I don't care if your demands are reasonable or not. I will not discuss anything with five hundred Communists and perverts!

BILLY We are more than five hundred!

HILTON I know there are thousands of people in this plant who will never go on strike.

REG Mr. Hilton, I can assure you that there are thousands who will.

NATE Who are you callin' a pervert?!

REG It's okay. I think we know where Mr. Hilton stands.

HILTON And you had better figure out on which side of the door you stand, Mr. Gibson. Good day gentlemen.

NATE Who's he callin' a pervert?!

The men begin to sing as they file out.

MEN

Oh, you can't blame us
We're workin' for the union,
We're workin' for the union,
We're workin' for the union.

Oh, you can't blame us
We're workin' for the union,
We're workin' for the union,
All day and night.

During the song, the set is decorated as the Union Hall. A banner reading "LOCAL 1005" is hung, a podium and a few chairs are brought in by the others. A union meeting is underway. REG is at the podium. There are shouts as REG is trying to bring order.

REG Hey, hey, hey, hey. All right!

LOUIS Order! Order!

REG Now look… look. I know all this talk of strike is scarin' a lot of people but it's the only way to get Hilton to recognize Local 1005!

Applause.

NATE That's right.

REG We will force him to negotiate! Our demands are reasonable. A nineteen-and-a-half cent an hour wage increase…

Uproar.

BILLY Hey! What happened to twenty-five cents increase?

REG Wait…. Wait… Charlie Millard and the Steelworkers think that our demands should be a little more reasonable.

BILLY We're givin' away the store!

LOUIS Come on, Billy!

ALICE We gotta stop bickering and get behind our negotiating team!

BILLY But there are no negotiations! We should strike now!

ROSE You're a single man, Billy! We have to put food on the table for our kids!

ALICE Let the union vote on it!

BILLY We'll get support from everyone in the city!

FRANK What difference does it make? The government's gonna take over the steel industry.

REG Is that what you want to happen?

LOUIS I heard we could be fined $5,000 a day for goin' on strike.

MARIE *(sarcastically)* Ya, and maybe get the death penalty.

LOUIS You askin' us to break the law, Reg?

REG Louis, it won't come to that. We intend to deal with Hugh Hilton, not the government.

ROSE I read that striking is against wartime regulations.

NATE There's lots of stuff that's against the law, Rosie.

BILLY *(frustrated)* Who cares about the law!

LOUIS I do!

ALICE gives a loud whistle to break up the bickering and order is restored.

ALICE Next order of business!

REG Look. There's more at stake here than a contract with Stelco. This is a struggle for change in the plant. It's a struggle for human dignity! I move that the voting commences now!

ALICE leaps to her feet and applauds. A few others follow her lead, some don't. During the next scenes voting continues as Steelworkers drop ballots into a box.

HILTON is in his office. KELLY paces nervously.

HILTON *(his voice rises in anger)* There is NOT going to be a strike!

KELLY I'm not so sure. The men believe they have legitimate complaints. Unfair treatment, unsafe working conditions…

HILTON It's all hogwash. Stories spread by a handful of dissidents. And I will not have any union imposed upon my employees against their will. Nobody's going to come in here and tell me how to run my steel mill!

KELLY Well, there do seem to be some problems with the workforce.

HILTON This is a steel company. It's hard, dirty work. But we pay good wages and we look after our employees.

KELLY I know that, Mr. Hilton, but what if it comes down to a strike? *(HILTON glares at her.)* A work stoppage.

HILTON We go on making steel. We'll bring in supplies by boat if we have to. By train! By airplane!

KELLY All right. So why don't we say something to the press like this. *(reads)* "In the event of an illegal walkout by a handful of dissident workers, Stelco will boldly carry on production with the help of loyal employees who make up the overwhelming majority of the workforce. We owe it to our family of steelworkers and the people of Canada."

She pauses and looks at HILTON.

HILTON That's bullshit, Miss Kelly.

KELLY That's public relations, Mr. Hilton.

Cross fade back to the union hall. Voters are lining up to put their ballots into a box on a table. NATE and ROSE have separated themselves from the group.

ROSE I clean houses all day, but I don't make enough to support you and the kids.

NATE If we get this raise you won't have to work.

ROSE Can't you stay out of the strike?

NATE No!

ROSE You could lose your job. We'll lose everythin'! How long do you think Mrs. Hilton will keep me on if you go out on strike?

NATE Mrs. Hilton? What the hell has she got to do with it?

ROSE I work for her. That's how I supported the family while you were away.

NATE Well now I'm back! So you quit!

ROSE And how do we eat if you go out? Where does the money come from?

NATE This is important! There is nothin' that's goin' to make me back down from the strike. Nothin'!

NATE moves away from ROSE. The lights cross fade to another part of the hall. REG and ALICE are watching the voters, and speaking privately.

ALICE You canna turn back now.

REG I never thought it would come to this, Alice.

ALICE D'you think you'll get the strike vote?

REG I don't know. But we have to make it sound like we will. It's a bit of a bluff.

ALICE And if you do get enough, the real question is how many workers will have the guts to walk.

REG You know, when we started this I knew what we were fighting for. But now… I don't know. It's a lot more complicated.

ALICE No it's not! You're fightin' for a fair dollar for a fair day's work. You're fightin' for respect for the workin' man!

REG *(mimics her Scottish accent)* Ach, that's it, is it dearie?

ALICE *(laughing)* Ach, an' so it is.

The lights cross fade, and reveal LOUIS and MARIE talking alone.

LOUIS Marie, the strike – it's comin'.

MARIE Ya.

LOUIS One of the guys on my shift, he's talkin' about stayin' in.

MARIE Stayin' in? What do you mean?

LOUIS Some of the men, they stay inside the mill, an' keep workin'.

MARIE Can they do that?

LOUIS They do what they want!

MARIE What are you gonna do?

LOUIS Me? I dunno. I go out, I can lose my job. We have to use our savings.

MARIE Ya?

LOUIS What about the house?

MARIE So we get it in ten years instead of five.

LOUIS You know, you not just a sweet Italian pastry.

LOUIS hugs her exuberantly. MARIE laughs.

REG sees FRANK crossing outside the union hall. He moves out to meet him.

REG Hey, hey, how's it goin', Frankie?

FRANK Oh, hi.

REG How come you missed the poker game on Friday?

FRANK Those aren't poker games any more, Reg. They're political meetin's.

REG It's gotta be that way. It looks like a strike's comin'.

FRANK Ya, well, I gotta go to work.

REG What are you gonna do? This strike is a chance for us to stand up for ourselves. To change this stinkin' place.

FRANK Don't lecture me!

REG It's important, Frank!

FRANK *(angrily)* Who the hell do you think you are? I'm your older brother!

The two men glare at each other for a long moment.

REG Remember we used to climb the bridges? An' you'd hold on to me? *(FRANK says nothing.)* I'm tryin' to hold onto you. To help everybody.

FRANK Shift's startin'.

FRANK exits. The lights cross fade.

HILTON and KELLY are talking in HILTON's office.

HILTON I don't think that union has enough support to organize a euchre party.

KELLY It might be closer than you think. We've got to be prepared.

HILTON The foremen say most of the men are going to stay in.

KELLY Those foremen are part of the problem. And they might be telling you what you want to hear.

HILTON The men are faithful to the company and to me.

KELLY Some of them are. But some of them might need convincing.

HILTON What are you suggesting?

KELLY The government has authorized a ten-cent an hour wage increase. Let's give that to the men who stay in, as soon as the strike starts. *(HILTON makes a gesture to object.) If* the strike starts.

HILTON Done.

KELLY There's something else. Those men will be locked inside the plant, twenty-four hours a day. Offer them triple time.

HILTON What?

KELLY The price of steel has just gone up five dollars a ton.

HILTON Yes, but triple time?

KELLY Twenty-four hours is three shifts. Think of it as regular time, round the clock. *(beat)* It might persuade more men to stay inside… on *our* side.

HILTON All right. I'll get a memo out to the Superintendents, and the Chairman of the Board. He'll love this.

KELLY He will.

HILTON and KELLY move forward to look down and watch the rally.

At the Union Hall, REG is making a speech to the assembled workers.

The unionists celebrate the strike vote while Hilton and Kelly watch.
l to r: Caden Douglas, Tim Campbell, Ryan Hollyman, Stephanie McNamara, Paolo Mancini, Lina Giornofelice, Tara Hughes. *balcony:* Kate Henning, Brian Paul.
photo by Roy Timm

REG We have the results of the plant vote: 3,114 in favour. And only 80 opposed!

Cheers.

The company has been trying to break the union for months now, and they have the government on their side, but the workers have finally spoken. *(cheers)* We HAVE a union! *(cheers)* We WANT human dignity! *(cheers)*

EVERYONE *(shouting)* HIT THE BRICKS!!

The men and women face the audience, watching the parade of workers and their families as they march by.

NATE There must be five, six thousand people!

REG Fillin' the streets! Marchin' past the Wilcox Gate!

LOUIS All together! Strong, united!

More voices have joined in. The volume is increasing.

MARIE There's men I never thought would be union!

BILLY Poles, Russians, Italians, English! All equal!

ROSE Big steelworkers cryin'!

NATE It's all about the things we're fightin' for!

ALICE We're gonna stay together and win this!

REG We won't give up, no matter what!

BILLY We want it so bad we're ready to bleed for it!

BILLY starts the Union Song – "Which Side Are You On?" HILTON and KELLY watch from above.

Come all of you good workers
Good news to you I'll tell,
Of how that good old union
Has come in here to dwell.

BILLY is joined by others as they are available.

My daddy was a Steel Man,
And I'm a Steel Man's son,
And I'll stick with the union
Till every battle's won.

UNIONISTS

Which side are you on?
Which side are you on?
Which side are you on?
Which side are you on?

The group has parted into two groups, as FRANK enters with a bag. He stops and looks at REG and the others. REG sees him and gestures to FRANK to join them. FRANK turns away, and walks through the gates into the mill. The gates close behind him. The song comes to a triumphant ending.

Split vocals as indicated:

BILLY Don't scab for the bosses,
WOMEN Don't listen to their lies,
MEN Us poor folks haven't got a chance
BILLY Unless we organize.

WOMEN Which side are you on?
MEN Which side are you on?
ALL Which side are you on?

ACT TWO

The soundscape of the mill begins in the darkness. It gradually changes into a rhythm which turns into the melody of the song. The lights come up as the cast enters. They begin to set up the picket line in front of the gate into the plant. Two of the men bring in a table. Others bring materials to make picket signs, as well as a few boxes, and a small riser to make a stage. Some are marching with signs; some are making signs as they sing. They are happy, filled with determination and resolve.

STRIKERS

The union is behind us,
We shall not be moved.
The union is behind us,
We shall not be moved.

Just like a tree that's standing by the water,
We shall not be moved.

We're fighting for our freedom,
We shall not be moved.
We're fighting for our freedom,
We shall not be moved.

Just like a tree that's standing by the water,
We shall not be moved.

REG and ALICE are making signs at a table. REG looks up and sees FRANK looking down at them from inside the mill. ALICE sees him as well. The song continues under the next lines.

ALICE How long can they stay in there?

REG I don't know. But the night before we struck they were haulin' in supplies by the truckload.

ALICE Firestone and Westinghouse are out on strike, and nobody's crossin' their picket lines. But Stelco is different. The men that stayed inside are scabbin' for Hughie Hilton.

Strikers parade on the picket line while Frank watches from inside the plant.
l to r: Paolo Mancini, Caden Douglas, Ryan Hollyman, George Masswohl, Tara Hughes, Stephanie McNamara, Lina Giornofelice, Tim Campbell.
photo by Roy Timm

NATE carries a bundle of signs.

NATE I was sure that all the guys on my team were comin' out with me. But I was wrong. Half those pricks scabbed.

ALICE Maybe some of them will come out, when they see us here.

STRIKERS

We're fighting for our union,
We shall not be moved.
We're fighting for our union,
We shall not be moved.

Just like a tree that's standing by the water,
We shall not be moved.

BILLY and LOUIS are marching with signs in front of the gate. The song continues.

BILLY We marched down to the gate and a lot of us broke out and started gettin' mad. We were gonna go in there and grab those scabs and drag them out, but the union ordered us back. I tell you, we coulda' won 'er right there.

LOUIS Bilko, he work in there forty years. He was sure that if he go out, Stelco not gonna hire him back. But he say to me, he say, "Louis, if you go out, I'm goin' out too!"

STRIKERS

We'll build a mighty union,
We shall not be moved.
We'll build a mighty union,
We shall not be moved.

Just like a tree that's standing by the water,
We shall not be moved.

MARIE and ROSE are sitting on wooden boxes folding pamphlets. LOUIS exits, moving further down the line. The song continues.

ROSE You know, the day Nate went out I lost half my cleaning jobs. I'd been with some of those ladies for years and they just slammed the door in my face.

MARIE I don't think it'll last long. There's not enough men inside, and they're losin' millions of dollars. Crazy old Hilton won't let it go on.

ROSE Funny, you know, Mrs. Hilton is one of the few ladies who kept me on. All she cares about is that I do my job, and do it well.

MARIE Louis says it's not just about jobs. He's fightin' Stelco to get some respect, and I'm right behind him.

The song has ended. BILLY has a brick in his hand.

BILLY All right everyone. Time to give Hilton a little demonstration of our strength.

NATE Let 'er go!

BILLY runs toward the gate to throw the brick. REG intercepts BILLY and stops him. He takes the brick out of his hand.

REG Hey now, come on, Billy. This is goin' to be a peaceful, orderly picket. Nate, just follow the union directions and make out the signs.

NATE *(reading the signs)* "1005 on strike." "Support our strikers." What is this crap? It should be, "Hang Hugh Hilton and pin him to the wall."

REG We don't want to look like we're out of control. We have people comin'. Alice, what time is Sam Lawrence comin'?

ALICE In a few minutes.

MARIE Reg, the food committee needs to know how many guys are goin' to be at each of the gates.

REG I don't know, Marie. Just do the best you can, okay?

LOUIS comes running in.

LOUIS Hey! The guys, they say there's over two thousand scabs in the plant. They gonna continue production.

MARIE Two thousand?

NATE That's impossible.

REG Ya, don't believe anythin' you hear.

ALICE It's all Hilton propaganda.

They continue to march. Cross fade to HILTON in his office. KELLY comes in.

HILTON Kelly, why did you talk to the press?

KELLY You can't shut them out, Mr. Hilton. You have to be open and accessible.

HILTON To hell with them!

KELLY The Board of Directors wants you to soften your image.

HILTON You can't be soft and win a fight with steelworkers, damn it.

KELLY I want you to call a press conference and make a statement directly to the newspapers.

HILTON I don't have time.

KELLY Have a look at this.

HILTON What is it?

KELLY Read it out loud. Believe me, you need the practice.

HILTON *(reading awkwardly)* "This is a democratic country and a man can live where he pleases and work where he pleases."

KELLY No, no, no. You have to do it convincingly, even friendly.

HILTON Friendly?

KELLY You're trying to sell something. You should speak to each member of the press as if you know him.

HILTON I do know them. They're jackals.

KELLY But if you act as if you like them, they'll listen, and maybe they'll sympathize. Look… try delivering it to me.

HILTON "This is a democratic country. A man can live where he pleases and work where he pleases. Under that freedom…"

KELLY Friendly—

HILTON *(forces a smile)* "Under that freedom he has the right to go on strike and he has the right to go to work."

KELLY Yes, much better. Try standing… in a friendly way.

HILTON *(He stands.)* "Stelco has a responsibility to those who want to work. And to those companies and families who need our continued support. Therefore, after hours of meetings with our loyal workers, we have decided that we must keep the Hamilton plant open."

KELLY Well done.

HILTON This is good. I believe it.

KELLY And so will they. We want the press to see us as reasonable. We're carrying on production. We're asking those that are on strike to come back to work. That sort of stance is bound to get us public support.

HILTON This could help.

KELLY That's the idea. So you'll talk to the press?

HILTON Can't we just send them this?

He indicates the paper he was reading from. KELLY throws her hands in the air in exasperation.

The strikers are parading around the picket line with signs. BILLY climbs up onto the scaffolding to look for Sam LAWRENCE.

REG *(calling to BILLY)* Can you see him?

BILLY Not yet.

ALICE *(calling)* He said he'd come.

BILLY *(calling)* Oh wait. There he is!

LOUIS Who's comin'?

MARIE Sam Lawrence. The mayor!

ALICE It's so good t' have the mayor be a labour man. Think a' the press we'll get.

REG & NATE *(singing to the tune of "Glory, Glory Hallelujah")*
We'll hang Hugh Hilton from the old apple tree,
He will see that Local 1005 will make the country free.

EVERYONE
We will break his nasty spirit and destroy his tyranny
For the Union makes us strong.

Sam LAWRENCE enters as the song turns into the union anthem of "Solidarity Forever." The mayor shakes hands as the song continues.

(chorus) Solidarity forever!
Solidarity forever!
Solidarity forever!
For the Union makes us strong!

Cheers. LAWRENCE steps up on a soap box. He speaks with a London working class accent.

LAWRENCE Thank you. Thank you. Alice, thank you very much for your invitation. Reg, good to see you again. Marie. It's encouraging to see so many women on the picket line.

MARIE And you too, Mister Mayor.

ALICE We're happy to see you support the strikers, sir.

LAWRENCE I'm a labour man first and the Chief Magistrate of this city second.

Cheers.

I'm one hundred percent behind the workers in this struggle. Victory will be ours.

STRIKERS Hip hip, hooray!

KELLY has come in and stands on the outskirts of the group. The strikers have not seen her before and do not understand the role she is playing in the strike.

KELLY But what about the men inside the plant? Aren't they your constituents too?

LAWRENCE Well, of course. I'm sure there are one or two Hamiltonians in there.

A few laugh.

KELLY Then will you open the picket line so the men can go home at night?

LAWRENCE That's not up to me, dear. I'm sure the union leaders would like to keep this a peaceful job action.

BILLY *(shaking his fist)* They gotta get past me!

NATE I got a present for 'em!

LAWRENCE As you can see, these men and women would be very happy to discuss the issues with the men inside.

Laughter and cheers.

KELLY But will the city guarantee the safety of those men?

LAWRENCE *(ignoring KELLY)* I want to wish all of you good folks the best of luck. Solidarity forever!

LAWRENCE waves goodbye and exits to more cheers. KELLY watches the crowd's enthusiasm.

STRIKERS Sam's our man! Sam's our man!

The men gather at the gates and call through to the scabs inside the plant. KELLY continues to watch.

BILLY You hear that, boys!?

REG We got the mayor out here!

The men bang their picket signs against the gates. They are getting angry.

NATE Let's get those scabs!

BILLY Come on out, scabs!

LOUIS The mayor. He want us to talk!

NATE Scabby bastards!

MEN *(chanting)* Scab! Scab! Scab!

The men's chanting continues as the women confer.

ALICE Looks like it's developin' to a wee bit o' trouble, gels.

MARIE What about that song?

ROSE Oh, I don't know. It's not ready.

ALICE Come on, dearie. You'll be fine.

They move to the stage. MARIE pulls LOUIS and NATE from the crowd of men. She speaks to them and they run to find their instruments. REG sets up boxes for a stage. ROSE brings a microphone.

MARIE *(calling to the men inside the plant)* Hey boys! We got somethin' for ya!

ALICE Somethin' for the scabs!

ROSE Unless they've scabbed over!

LOUIS enters with his accordion and NATE with his guitar. KELLY exits during the song. The three women sing the "Scab Song" in the style of the Andrews Sisters.

WOMEN

We're out to join our brothers,
Along with many others,
While the scabs get great big pay.
And for a decent living,
That Stelco isn't giving
We picket the days away.

The scabs are getting dirty.
No wife to wash their shirty,
And their clothes do smell they say.
They must be getting tired.
The company has them hired
Twenty-four long hours a day.

A scab is a fellow
Who is mighty yellow,
Disliked by all the town.
Hilton says you're loyal,
But you're really going to boil,
When he finally lets you down.

So the big shots keep talking,
To keep the scabs from walking
In the picket lines we know.
You're going to regret it
Because we will not forget it.
You're scabs wherever you go.

The song ends with whistles and shouts from the men. KELLY and HILTON are talking in HILTON's office.

HILTON Look, Kelly, I don't see why I have to go to this parliamentary inquiry.

KELLY Because in the public's eye you are Stelco. You have to state the company's case.

HILTON Everybody knows my position. The strike's been going on for three long weeks and I want to be here when the damned Steelworkers' Union collapses.

KELLY But the parliamentary inquiry has the ear of the Prime Minister.

HILTON Mackenzie King does nothing. He spends most of his time talking to his mother.

KELLY Would she be pro- or anti-strike?

HILTON This strike's illegal. They should bring in the police. Let them do the dirty work.

KELLY There won't be any dirty work. The point of the inquiry is to show we're being fair to the…

HILTON *Fair*? What's fair got to do with it? I've got a steel company to run.

KELLY You have to go up to Ottawa and explain that there is anarchy in Hamilton. We need their support. King must be worried about losing votes.

HILTON I got a call from him last night. He said he'd have to ask his dog.

KELLY Isn't that dog dead?

HILTON So is his mother!

Cross fade to ALICE and REG, walking on the picket line. NATE and BILLY are playing cards.

REG What's all this parliament nonsense?

ALICE It's all a bit of a show, with a bunch of MPs sittin' around, and they talk and they talk. It makes it look like they're doin' somethin'.

REG But if they send in the Mounties…

NATE Let 'em try.

REG We can't fight the company and the cops.

BILLY What's a little blood?

ALICE We want this to be a peaceful strike.

BILLY This is a struggle to the end, Alice.

LOUIS comes running in.

LOUIS Hey, anyone see Marie?

ALICE She's over by the other gate.

LOUIS What she doin' there?

ALICE Servin' sandwiches on the line.

BILLY Chattin' up the men.

NATE Entertainin' the troops.

NATE and BILLY laugh.

REG Hey Louis. Are there any Italian scabs?

LOUIS No way. Italians are strong. We stick together.

MARIE comes in.

Marie, where you been?

MARIE I was down at the other gate talkin' to scabs, and I got two to come over the fence.

LOUIS How you do that?

MARIE Well I told them that their wives were havin' a lot of late night visitors, and they weren't Fuller Brush men.

The others laugh. ALICE and REG exit. LOUIS pulls MARIE aside.

LOUIS You go down there by yourself, Marie?

MARIE Ya, by myself.

LOUIS What about all those guys?

MARIE What's the matter, Louis? You jealous?

LOUIS No, but I don' like you hangin' around them guys. You stay up here so I can keep an eye on you.

MARIE What are you talkin' about? I'm helpin' with the food. I have to go down there.

LOUIS Not any more you don't. Let someone else do it.

MARIE You're crazy! Don't you trust me?

LOUIS No! And I don' trust those guys either.

MARIE What can happen in broad daylight?

LOUIS Nothin' gonna happen 'cause you' gonna be right here with me!

MARIE Who do you think you're married to, Mamma Bravo?

LOUIS Your mamma wouldn' be out there laughin' and jokin' with other guys!

MARIE You *are* jealous!

LOUIS AM NOT!

MARIE Then don't go on and on any more. It's my strike too!

LOUIS I know! But you mind me!

MARIE You mind me too. *Capiche?*

LOUIS turns and walks away. MARIE makes an "up yours" gesture behind LOUIS' back.

ALICE rushes in. She is out of breath.

ALICE Nora-Frances Henderson is on her way here! She's comin' to cross the picket line.

NATE What?

ALICE People down the line seen her. Something about seein' the poor scabs inside.

BILLY *(alarmed)* She's not crossin' *this* line!

NATE Over my dead body!

LOUIS Who she think she is?

ALICE She's a bloody-minded City Controller. She's got a lot of influence.

BILLY She ain't gonna use it here.

HENDERSON enters with a photographer. She is mid-forties, a bit frumpy, wearing an odd hat. She speaks with a middle-class English accent.

ALICE Is it that you're thinkin' of crossing the picket line, Controller?

HENDERSON I intend to show that this city will not bow to mob rule. When loyal employees cannot go to work in safety, then I will fight to protect their rights.

MARIE And what rights have been violated?

HENDERSON Men have been savagely beaten. Their property vandalized. Their families threatened. I intend to do something about it.

BILLY Are you prepared for violence against yourself?

HENDERSON Yes, I am prepared.

The strikers have gathered shoulder to shoulder to block her from entering the gate. Their voices rise angrily. HENDERSON stands defiantly in front of them.

NATE Nobody crosses this line!

MARIE We're not afraid!

BILLY Block the gate!

NATE Ya, right!

LOUIS Don' let her pass!

The group holding picket signs as they chant.

STRIKERS
Go home, Nora! Go home, Nora!
Go home, Nora! Go home, Nora!

REG runs in and holds up his arms for quiet. The photographer takes pictures.

REG Hold on! Hold on!

HENDERSON I demand access to the Steel Company of Canada.

REG By all means, Miss Henderson.

Beat.

HENDERSON I beg your pardon?

REG Right this way. Step aside, guys. Let her through. Come on. Would you like me to escort you through the gate, Miss Henderson?

HENDERSON I can manage quite well on my own, thank you very much.

BILLY moves to block HENDERSON from entering.

Get out of my way!

REG Billy!

Beat. After a moment BILLY moves aside and HENDERSON enters through the gate. The PHOTOGRAPHER goes to follow her and NATE blocks his way.

NATE Where the hell do you think you're goin', bud?

PHOTOGRAPHER I'm takin' pictures.

NATE There'll be a picture of you in the hospital if you try and go through that line!

NATE grabs the PHOTOGRAPHER's arm and forcefully steers him off the stage. Then NATE rejoins the others.

BILLY *(angrily to REG)* You shouldn't've let her through, Reg!

REG Hey, hey. What harm can she do? It's the only way to handle it.

BILLY But it's the principle of the thing. Nobody crosses the line!

REG Billy, she is a force in this town.

ALICE The last thing that we need is her tellin' the press that she was right all along. That the people on the line are violent hooligans.

NATE grabs BILLY and pulls him away. The two of them look back at the others, unhappy with the development.

MARIE Good thinking, Reg.

LOUIS What she gonna do in there, anyway?

MARIE Nothin'. She wouldn't know the difference between a steel mill and a light bulb.

ALICE Ach, there's an election coming up and her constituents aren't exactly the Clydeside working class. She'll get lots of votes for this.

LOUIS She's a witch.

MARIE Here she comes!

HENDERSON comes out through the gates and is greeted by all of the strikers.

REG Did you find what you were looking for, Miss Henderson?

HENDERSON I found the men contented, vigorous and cheerful.

BILLY Ya. A nice bunch of scabs we've got.

HENDERSON It sickens me that these workers cannot have access to and egress from their place of work.

ALICE & MARIE *(mocking)* Oh, egress…

REG They can have egress from the plant any time they like.

HENDERSON Yes, but can they go back inside?

NATE They can try.

HENDERSON I intend to approach the Board of Police Commissioners to guarantee their safe passage.
If the Board refuses me, I shall bring the issue to City Council.

She begins to walk off and NATE stands in front of her. She tries to dodge around him and NATE blocks her again. She looks at him sternly and NATE finally steps aside and she exits.

NATE Okay, Nora.

MARIE Bye bye, Nora.

ALICE Toodledoo, Nora.

BILLY Don't be a stranger!

MARIE Ah. They wouldn't dare sic the cops on us. Would they?

REG We'll get on to Sam Lawrence about it. Everyone back on the line now.

The others join the line, marching. NATE kicks his picket sign in frustration. REG picks it up and goes to him.

What's the matter with you?

NATE I'm sick and tired of walkin' around in circles. We gotta do somethin'.

REG Look, Nate. I heard that the union's organizin' a navy.

NATE A navy?

REG The company's bringin' supplies to the scabs by boat across the bay.

NATE Bastards!

REG The union's got ahold of an old rumrunner, the *Whisper*. She's a speed boat that can do thirty-five knots, the fastest thing on the bay. They're lookin' for a crew.

NATE Ya?

REG They need guys that aren't afraid.

NATE *(laughing)* Shit kickin' time! *(He begins to run out.)*

REG *(calling after him)* Hey Nate, come on now, eh? No rough stuff. Just scare 'em off.

NATE Ya, right!

NATE is gone. REG and the others move upstage. Cross fade to ROSE in her apartment. She is listening to the radio.

CHML ...was reported to have been rammed by the Union boat, the *Whisper*. One man remains in critical but stable condition at Hamilton General Hospital.

ROSE turns off the radio. She holds her head in her hands. NATE enters.

NATE *(shouting)* Rosie! Ha. Rosie you shoulda seen it. Boom! Splash. Splash. Then nothin' but a hat floatin' in the water.

ROSE I heard it already.

NATE How?

ROSE The radio.

NATE No shit! *(laughs)*

ROSE One of the men is in the hospital. They don't know if he's going to make it.

NATE Ya, well, that'll teach those guys who they're dealin' with.

ROSE What's the matter with you? You used to drink with those guys. Now you're trying to kill them?

NATE No one's gettin' killed. Just a little wet, maybe.

ROSE I don't know how you can joke about it.

NATE I'm not jokin' about it.

ROSE Maybe you can tell Bobby and see how funny he thinks it is.

NATE What are you talkin' about?

ROSE Your son! He's lying up there with broken ribs! He called somebody's father a scab, and six kids jumped him. The police brought him home.

NATE He knows how to take care of himself.

ROSE That's all you think about, isn't it? Drinkin' and fightin' and bein' with your buddies. Bobby is thirteen years old. He needs a father, and he gets you tellin' him to fight his way through everything!

NATE I don't need this.

ROSE Well, we don't need you. I've had it! You're never here! You can't even support your family, but you expect me to keep working so you can get drunk every night! You should hear what they call you behind your back.

NATE Knock it off!

NATE grabs her by the arm. ROSE slaps his face. Beat.

ROSE Get out of here! GET OUT!

NATE exits, and ROSE turns away from him.

Cross fade to HILTON's office. KELLY is at a microphone, and FRANK and HILTON are standing by. A radio jingle of "Roll Out the Barrel" is heard over the speakers.

SONG
Roll out the sheet steel,
We'll make the sheet mill run.
Roll out the sheet, boys,
Workers are all having fun.

KELLY reads from a script in front of a microphone.

KELLY Tonight on S-C-A-B radio we have Canada's biggest family, broadcasting from Slag Mountain Lodge, inside the heart of Stelco. This program is produced by the men who have stayed inside to keep Stelco alive. We start off tonight's broadcast with a special feature with mill worker Frank Gibson. Good evening, Frank.

FRANK is very awkward and nervous to be on radio.

FRANK *(He isn't close enough to the microphone.)* Evenin'. *(KELLY pulls him closer to the microphone)* Oh.... Evening.

KELLY Could you tell everybody why you decided to stay inside, Frank, and continue to work?

FRANK Stelco's done a lot for me.

FRANK is not reading his script. KELLY points to it.

KELLY Do you think the strikers are encouraged by the triple time wages they're being offered?

FRANK continues to ignore his script.

FRANK They're steelworkers. They won't back down without a fight.

Frank and Kelly perform for "scab radio" while Hilton looks on.
l to r: Kate Henning, Brian Paul, George Masswohl.
photo by Roy Timm

KELLY waves her copy of the script at FRANK in frustration.

KELLY We have learned that the strike is at the point of collapse.

FRANK I want it to be over, same as everybody. There's good men on both sides.

KELLY Tell me, Frank. What does S-C-A-B stand for?

KELLY points to his script.

FRANK *(sarcastically)* "Stelco Continues Along Boldly".... Is that what you want me to say?

KELLY, desperate, switches into a radio pitchman's voice.

KELLY That's right, Frank. Thank you for that insight.

She pushes FRANK away from the microphone.

That was Mr. Frank Gibson, ladies and gentlemen, a man who is standing up for the principles he believes in. Mr. Hilton would be proud of you, Frank.

FRANK backs off, shaking his head.

And speaking of our fearless leader. I am proud to introduce to you now that old steelworker himself, Mister Hugh Hilton.

HILTON shakes his head "No."

Ladies and gentlemen, Mr. Hilton is making his way to the microphone now, shaking the hands of his faithful supporters.

HILTON points his finger in anger at KELLY.

HILTON *(whispering)* I said no. *(KELLY covers the mike with her papers.)*

KELLY *(whispering)* You also said "no bullshit."

KELLY offers him a paper with his speech on it. HILTON reluctantly takes the paper. He moves up to the mike.

HILTON *(reading)* "Thank you. Thank you. Almost two thousand steelworkers are under siege in this plant and the numbers are growing every day. These people are doing a tremendous job in upholding the law and supporting our…"

HILTON pauses and drops the script to his side. He speaks sincerely.

I don't want to read this. *(beat)* I want to say thank you to all the men who have stayed in, standing behind the company in this fight. I know how difficult it is for you, under the threat of violence, not to be able to return to your homes, and your wives, and I know how difficult it is on your families. But you and I believe that a man has the right to work where he wants, and when he wants. We're going to win this battle with your help. Thank you.

KELLY is moved by his heartfelt message. She tries to shake HILTON's hand in congratulations, but he storms away from her. The play-out jingle is to the tune of "Deep in the Heart of Texas."

SONG
The furnace is bright,
The mills are light,
Deep in the heart of Stelco.

Our steel is just fine
All of the time,
Deep in the heart of Stelco.

KELLY watches him go.

Cross fade to MARIE and LOUIS who are walking the picket line. NATE and BILLY are working on something in a corner.

MARIE I don't know if I can do this anymore.

LOUIS What you talkin' about?

MARIE All I do is make sandwiches. Thousands of them. And spaghetti. I can't eat any more, I'm so sick of food.

LOUIS But the guys on the line gotta eat! You and the other girls, you keepin' us goin'.

MARIE Ya, well I'm tellin' you. I don't know how long I can keep it up!

LOUIS You make the food! That's your part.

They walk along in silence. MARIE is fuming.

MARIE And we gotta talk about Nate.

LOUIS What about him?

MARIE He's a pig.

LOUIS Marie!

MARIE He is! We've only been on our own three months, finally away from Mamma and Poppa, and now we have him sleepin' on the couch!

LOUIS Ya, well, he's in trouble.

MARIE Let him take his trouble somewhere else.

LOUIS He's my friend.

MARIE I don't care. He comes in all hours. Day and night!

LOUIS He and Rosie, they work it out.

MARIE We have no privacy!

LOUIS Where's he gonna go?

MARIE Tell him to go home! Go anywhere. I don't care. Just get him out!

LOUIS I'm not tellin' him nothin'!

MARIE is even more annoyed. They walk along in silence again.

MARIE Well, sometimes, I think, he's lookin' at me.

LOUIS Who is?

MARIE Nate. Your friend! In our house!

LOUIS looks across the picket line at NATE and BILLY.

LOUIS *(quietly) Va fangul.*

LOUIS storms across the stage toward NATE. NATE and BILLY have rigged up a big slingshot that they operate using their feet and arms. They are using it to fire rocks into the plant from the picket line. LOUIS approaches.

NATE Let her go, Billy!

BILLY Catch this, you scabs!

BILLY lets a rock go. We hear the sound of a window smashing. BILLY and NATE laugh.

LOUIS What are you doin'?

NATE Sendin' a little message to the scabs.

LOUIS Reg won't like it.

BILLY To hell with Reg. Those scabs are laughin' at us.

BILLY places another rock in the slingshot.

LOUIS *(to NATE)* Hey. What are you doin' with Marie?

NATE Whatcha mean?

LOUIS She say you been lookin' at her.

NATE What? I never looked, Louis, that's crazy!

LOUIS *(shouting)* Just get your stuff outta our place!

NATE You gonna believe…

LOUIS I know the sort a guy you are!

BILLY lets another rock go, another smash. He laughs and cheers. REG comes running in.

REG What's goin' on here?

BILLY We're fightin' back, Reg.

NATE Louis's bein' an asshole.

LOUIS Me an asshole?

REG Billy, if there's any violence the police are gonna move in.

BILLY To hell with the police. We gotta stand up for ourselves.

REG We don't need to hurt people and damage property to win this.

LOUIS *(pointing at NATE)* You talk to him about hurtin' people!

NATE To hell with you!

BILLY We're not winnin' nothin'!

REG Just knock it off! All of you!

NATE This is bullshit!

BILLY The strike is goin' nowhere your way!

REG We have to stick together!

LOUIS Together with him!?

BILLY Nowhere!

NATE To hell with it!

NATE runs off. BILLY follows him. LOUIS storms off the other direction. REG is left wondering what happened.

MARIE and ALICE watch the men running off and then they talk quietly.

MARIE I woke up the other night screaming. Louis was standin' over me, his eyes poppin' out of his head.

ALICE We've all been havin' nightmares.

MARIE I was alone in this huge factory, standin' at this never-ending assembly line, as far as you could see: baloney, bread, baloney, bread. Suddenly the bread line started speeding up, and I couldn't keep up with the baloney, and I started screaming at the machine but it wouldn't stop. All I could think about was the hundreds of picketers rippin' into their sandwiches and finding... no baloney.

ALICE Sounds like me with the groceries. Come on. We have to fill some more bags.

The women exit. NATE and BILLY run on, panting.

BILLY Wait! Wait.

NATE This is bullshit.

BILLY What was that about?

NATE Louis? Ah, I been stayin' at their place. I guess it's a little small.

BILLY Did Rose throw you out?

NATE *(He nods.)* She never gives me a break.

BILLY You're gonna go back though, eh?

NATE I really miss the kids.

BILLY It's just this stupid doin' nothin'. Walkin' around and around. It's makin' everyone crazy.

NATE Ya…

BILLY We gotta do somethin' if we want to win this. Somethin' big.

NATE Like what?

BILLY I don't know, but I'm workin' on it. Listen, you can stay at my place, if you don't got anywhere to go.

NATE I might have to. Marie – she's been lookin' at me kinda funny.

BILLY Then you better get outta there!

They laugh, and exit.

REG and LOUIS are marching on the line with signs.

REG Because Frank is scabbin' on the inside, I gotta work twice as hard as anyone else on the line.

LOUIS You gonna kill yourself, Reg.

REG The men are gettin' really antsy. Lots of the guys are blamin' the union 'cause nothin's happening, and then I get in trouble for tryin' to control the violence.

LOUIS Maybe you gotta let it happen.

REG It's not the way to go, but some of them won't stop. I'm stuck in the middle.

LOUIS We're all stuck.

They continue to march. Cross fade to ALICE down right with BILLY. She is stuffing grocery bags.

ALICE I think you could be doin' somethin' other than tryin' to smash things up.

BILLY It's time to get somethin' going, comrade.

ALICE You'll get yourself in jail, Billy. An' how's that helpin' the union cause?

BILLY It'd put pressure on Hilton to settle this thing. Might get us some attention.

ALICE Not the right kind. You need to get away from the line. Come an' help me deliver groceries. We've been getting all kinds of food donated. Food that we're giving out to the wives and families of the strikers.

BILLY That's work for the women.

ALICE Oh that's a great thing for a Communist to say. "Helping the less fortunate.... That's women's work." You take these groceries to Myrtle. Frank Gibson's Myrtle.

BILLY I'm not helpin' a scab's family.

ALICE Look, Billy, Frankie an' Myrtle were good to our family when we had hard times.

BILLY Then you do it.

ALICE I canna do it. Reg'd never let me. But I'm worried about Myrtle. You get over there and see how she's doing.

BILLY I don't know.

ALICE *(smiling at him)* You'll do it to help me, won't you? That's a boy.

REG enters the area.

REG Whatcha got him doin' now?

ALICE Billy was just promisin' me he'd help out some of the families with the groceries.

REG That's great, kid. Thanks.

BILLY reluctantly leaves with two bags of groceries.

ALICE We've got to get him off the line. All he does is prowl around lookin' for trouble.

REG A lot of the men want to go into the plant and haul out the scabs and... *(REG holds up a fist as if about to punch someone.)* It's all I can do to hold them back.

ALICE looks around to make sure no one is listening. She speaks in a hushed voice.

ALICE I dunna know what we're gonna do about the mortgages, Reggie.

REG Did you have that meeting?

ALICE I haven't got the heart to tell the others yet. Up 'til now I've been able to sweet-talk the mortgage people into bein' lenient with the strikers. But they put in a new manager, and he's hard line. He won't listen to worker's knock-knock jokes, or hear stories about their families. He told me they're goin' to start to foreclose.

REG No!

ALICE I begged with him, I pleaded, I threatened to withdraw all of the union business, but it was no use.

REG And?

ALICE They're goin' to call the loans, an' one of the first ones on the list is ours.

REG Shit!

ALICE Yes, shit indeed. I dunna know what we're gonna do, Reggie. Where are we goin' to go? *(She cries, and REG takes her in his arms.)*

Cross fade to HILTON and KELLY in his office.

HILTON Kelly!

KELLY I'm right here.

HILTON I just got off the phone with our dauntless Prime Minister.

KELLY What are they going to do?

HILTON Nothing.

KELLY Nothing? But…

HILTON Not a damned thing. The Parliamentary Inquiry was just a stall. We're going to have to fight this thing out by ourselves.

KELLY No, we could try shipping by boat again.

HILTON We had the *Whisper* impounded by the police, but they'd just find another one.

KELLY What about the airplanes?

HILTON The union's got their own plane and it's buzzing ours. From now on we are playing this game *my* way.

KELLY I don't like the sound of that.

HILTON Hardball, Kelly. That's the only thing steelworkers understand.

KELLY The Board will not support this.

HILTON To hell with them. *(shouting into the phone)* Get me transportation!

KELLY I cannot approve any violence against – anything that might blacken the image of the company.

HILTON I'm going to blacken something!

KELLY You're going to break through the line?

HILTON You're bloody right I am! We're going to break this strike wide open.

KELLY Mr. Hilton!

HILTON Are you with me or against me?

They are in a stand-off.

Cross fade to MARIE and ALICE arriving at ROSE's place with bags of groceries.

MARIE Hello, Rose.

ALICE How you doin'?

ROSE I'm just on my way out.

ALICE Aye. Well, we just thought we'd be bringin' you some of these groceries.

MARIE We've got all kinds of good stuff.

ROSE Thanks, but I'm sure other people need it more than I do.

MARIE It's not charity, Rose. We're all sharin' it.

ALICE We're drownin' in cabbages that the farmers have given us.

ROSE My kids don't like cabbage.

MARIE Well we don't want to waste good food. Make cabbage rolls. I'll bet they'll eat cabbage rolls.

MARIE thrusts one of the packages into ROSE's arms. She takes it reluctantly. The others are deposited on a chair.

ROSE Thank you.

ROSE puts the package with the others.

ALICE So how are the wee ones?

ROSE Fine.

ALICE You know, Rose, we miss seeing your smilin' face. What've you been doin'?

Beat.

ROSE I haven't left the house in three weeks. I clean it every day. Scrub the floor. Polish the windows. The only adult voice I hear is on the radio. *(beat)* I'm fine.

ALICE Why don't you come down to the line? We need all the help we can get.

MARIE You could work makin' sandwiches with me.

ROSE Oh, I see. This is an official visit.

ALICE No, no, it's not that. It's just that we thought you might need to get out and see your old friends.

MARIE Nate spends all his time on the picket line. You'd have a chance of maybe…

ROSE Is he still staying with you?

MARIE No. He had to move.

ROSE Up to his old shenanigans was he?

ALICE Rose, you'd be so proud of him. He's on the line day and night.

ROSE Ya, well that's Nate, always findin' an excuse for a party.

MARIE He's workin' for the union.

ROSE You can take your union and shove it.

MARIE What's the matter with you? Nate's on strike to make a better life for your family!

ROSE He's never done anythin' for anybody but himself.

MARIE He's doing this for you!

ALICE Marie!

MARIE What?

ALICE Shut it!

MARIE turns away. ALICE tries one last appeal.

ALICE *(gently)* Rosie, come down to the line and see for yourself.

ROSE I don't want to see him again.

ALICE You don't mean that.

MARIE Are you through with him?

ROSE It's none of your bloody business!

ROSE turns and storms out, leaving ALICE and MARIE in her living room.

Cross fade to BILLY and REG on the line.

BILLY I've been takin' groceries to some a' the women. It's not as bad as I thought it would be.

REG I'm sure they're grateful for the help.

BILLY Some a' them sure are.

They walk in silence.

REG How's Nate doin?

BILLY Ah well, they found out that he was stayin' at my place, and I got kicked out. We both did.

REG Where are you stayin'?

BILLY We kind of just been sleepin' down by the plant gate. I was down here twenty-four hours a day anyway.

REG *(shaking his head)* How's that goin'?

BILLY We're startin' to get to them, Reg. On Sunday I was walkin' the line, and I saw one of the scabs sneakin' back over the fence. So I jumped up and grabbed hold of his ankles, an' his jacket gets caught on the wire, an' he's hangin' there like a scarecrow. *(BILLY rips the sign off his picket stick, and slams the stick against the fence.)* So I take my picket stick and WHAM! He was out like a light.

REG You gotta stop fightin', Billy.

REG pulls BILLY downstage, away from the fence.

BILLY Communists aren't afraid of action. You don't know 'cause you're at union meetin's all the time, but sometimes there's barely twelve guys on the line.

REG I know, but you can't win this thing that way.

BILLY But what about the trucks? They tried to move stuff through the line, and a whole gang of us threw a truck on its side.

REG I don't want to hear about it. That's exactly the kind of crap that is gonna get the police called in.

BILLY The cops won't come down on us.

REG Billy! The meeting is tonight. The city council is voting to bring in the police because of all the violence.

They turn upstage and walk into the meeting, already in full swing. Sam LAWRENCE is chairing the meeting and Nora-Frances HENDERSON is trying to speak. All of the strikers are at the meeting.

STRIKERS *(chanting)* Go home, Nora! Go home, Nora! Go home, Nora!

LAWRENCE ORDER! ORDER! *(the rabble grows quiet)* Now, Miss Henderson, your motion is to direct the police to maintain order on the Stelco picket line.

Boos and catcalls.

HENDERSON As you all know, this strike is against Canadian law. The men on the picket line are out of control. If council does not pass this motion and restore law and order, I despair of the future of our great city.

LAWRENCE But it is the considered opinion of the Chief of Police that the picket line is peaceful.

Cheers.

HENDERSON There are two thousand men locked inside that plant. It's disgraceful. Men have been beaten! Do you call that peaceful?

Boos. The hubbub increases.

NATE *(shaking his fist)* We'll show them scabs a new law!

REG *(trying to maintain order of the strikers)* Quiet down!

BILLY The scabs are takin' shots at us!

HENDERSON Men like you will end up behind bars unless you act in a civilized manner!

LOUIS Shut up, Nora!

LAWRENCE ORDER! ORDER! Only Councillors are allowed to speak!

Everyone boos and jeers at HENDERSON.

REG *(He gestures to calm the strikers.)* Settle down!

LAWRENCE *(banging his gavel)* ORDER! ORDER!

BILLY She's the one that's caused the trouble in this town.

LAWRENCE Miss Henderson, as Mayor of Hamilton I will not support any action that will bring strike breakers into this city!

HENDERSON Those men are being held hostage! The law is being violated!

ALICE What about us?

MARIE I'll violate *you*!

Everyone laughs, and boos HENDERSON.

LAWRENCE We have had a full debate on the issue, and I am going to call for the motion to be voted on. All in favour of bringing in police to maintain order on the line?

HENDERSON puts up her hand. Boos from the strikers.

LAWRENCE Opposed?

All the strikers and their wives put up their hands. LAWRENCE is counting the council members' votes.

Only Council members may vote the motion. It appears we have a tie.

More boos and jeers from the strikers.

As Mayor, I have the tie-breaking vote. And I vote NO! The motion is defeated.

The strikers explode in joy, cheering, waving signs and booing HENDERSON.

STRIKERS Go home, Nora! Go home, Nora!

(singing) We'll hang Nora-Frances from a sour apple tree.
Sour apple tree, sour apple tree,
We'll hang Nora-Frances from a sour apple tree
As we go marching on.

HENDERSON exits. The strikers follow her as they sing. Sam LAWRENCE exits, and the meeting disperses.

We'll hang Nora-Frances from a sour apple tree.
Sour apple tree, sour apple tree,
We'll hang Nora-Frances from a sour apple tree …

Suddenly BILLY runs off after HENDERSON with his picket sign stick. The singing stops.

REG NO, BILLY!

We hear a crowd of men yelling offstage.

ALICE Leave her alone!

LOUIS Look at them guys!

NATE She deserves it!

MARIE He's in real trouble now!

LOUIS Those damn Commies.

REG Let's get back to the line! Come on! Everybody back to the line!

REG manages to get the others moving and they go back to the line. NATE seems torn between BILLY and the others. The picketers parade in front of the gate with their signs.

ALICE What's wrong with Billy?

NATE There's nothin' wrong with him.

REG Come on, Nate.

MARIE That was nearly a riot.

LOUIS It's the Communists that organized it.

MARIE They'll bring in the cops for sure.

BILLY enters. He has a big smile, signalling he is proud of his accomplishments.

ALICE Billy, what have you done?

BILLY We didn't hurt her. Just rockin' her car.

NATE That'll shut her up.

LOUIS You and yer stupid Commie thugs!

REG Did you want to get arrested? Or get killed?

BILLY The company boys protected her.

NATE He didn't do nothin'!

REG Only hurt the Union.

LOUIS Little Commie bastard.

BILLY Come on, Wop!

REG holds LOUIS from attacking BILLY. NATE holds BILLY back. There is a fierce stand-off.

ALICE Billy!

REG Come on! Enough of this bullshit!

MARIE Louis, that's enough!

The strikers break off the confrontation. BILLY and NATE move down left. The others continue to parade about with their signs, but they look at BILLY and NATE suspiciously.

Cross fade to HILTON's office. He storms in. KELLY is waiting for him.

HILTON I tell you, Kelly, this is the end. The absolute finish! There's riots in the streets and the City of Hamilton will do nothing! NOTHING!

KELLY Maybe we should calm down.

HILTON Calm down? They attacked Nora-Frances! You'll never find a more honest citizen than her!

KELLY I've just been speaking to the Chairman of the Board…

HILTON I didn't build the Steel Company of Canada to see it taken over by a bunch of thugs and Communists!

KELLY And he agrees with me. He strongly recommends against the use of violence.

HILTON They don't understand anything else!

KELLY You don't understand! If you injure anyone it will strengthen the union. Public opinion will swing to their side!

HILTON To hell with the public! We're involved in a war, and you don't win a war without a fight!

KELLY Mr. Hilton. You have to think about these men and their families. I have been down on the line, watching them march, hearing them cheer for the people who support them. They deserve to be treated like humans. Not machines. I don't think it will be the end of the company.

HILTON What has happened to you? Have you gone over to the other side?

KELLY No, but the Board cannot and will not condone any use of violence or force. If you go forward with this, you go alone.

HILTON FINE! Get out of the way. I'm going to put an end to this, once and for all!

KELLY exits the office. HILTON picks up his phone.

Cross fade to LOUIS, MARIE, REG, and ALICE, walking the line. It is evening. BILLY and NATE enter down left. BILLY is holding a paper bag.

BILLY *(speaking to NATE)* We need action, or this strike will just shrivel up and die.

NATE So what're you gonna do? Go in and break some windows?

BILLY Somethin' bigger than that.

REG approaches BILLY and NATE. LOUIS comes over to listen.

REG I was wonderin' where you guys were.

BILLY I got a few things here for the scabs on the inside. You comin' with us?

REG No. I don't think so.

BILLY Why not?

LOUIS Shouldn't be doin' that kinda stuff.

BILLY You're listenin' to Reg too much.

NATE *(aside to BILLY)* Are you gonna cut cables? Sugar in gas tanks? Crap like that?

BILLY opens the paper bag, and shows NATE what's inside.

Shit! *(beat)* Ya.

BILLY moves toward the gate. NATE follows him.

REG What are you doin', Nate?

NATE We got somethin' to do.

REG What's more important than bein' on the line?

BILLY We're gonna lose this strike unless we take some action.

REG What kind of action?

NATE We're goin' into the plant.

BILLY A little bang for your buck.

REG grabs BILLY's arm.

REG What's in the bag, Billy?

BILLY Don't, Reg.

REG *(demanding)* What's in the bag!?

BILLY holds the bag away from REG. NATE takes the bag from his hand.

BILLY What's the matter, Reggie? You afraid little Frankie's gonna get hurt?

REG swings at BILLY, but BILLY dodges and punches REG in the gut. The women scream. NATE pulls BILLY away. LOUIS grabs REG. BILLY and NATE run off.

REG *(shouting)* Stop them!

ALICE *(shouting at REG)* What's the matter with you? You're no better than a common hoodlum.

REG What am I supposed to do?!

LOUIS lets go of REG. LOUIS and MARIE exit.

ALICE You don't fight. Violence is not the way.

REG I don't know. Maybe they're right.

ALICE Is that the kind of victory you want? Lowering yourself down to their kind of hooliganism?

REG My way isn't working, Alice!

ALICE Well, fightin' each other is not gonna win anythin'.

Beat.

REG *(He hangs his head.)* I don't think we are gonna win.

ALICE Don't say that! Don't even think that.

REG I think about it all the time.

ALICE Well, stop it. You've got to lead these men!

REG I am not leading anyone! No one listens to me. I got nothin' to say.

ALICE That's not true! You have led them out on strike, led them to stay out. Even when not one of them wanted to get out of bed, you made them come down here to the line.

REG You're the one that's been leading! Pushing me to stand up to them. "Get back out there," you'd tell me. "Get up and say somethin'!"

ALICE I never had to push you!

REG Oh, come on, Alice! None of this would have happened if it hadn't been for you.

ALICE You canna blame this on me.

REG Well, I didn't want it to go on this long. I didn't want to lose our house over it!

ALICE You think I did?

REG I don't know. I don't think anything would stop you! I can't!

ALICE Reggie!

REG No! I'm finished! You've been tellin' me what to do! Now you do it! Do whatever you want!

ALICE No!

REG storms off, leaving ALICE by herself on stage. She turns and exits the other way.

BILLY and NATE enter, moving along the fence. It's darker now.

NATE If we go in here, they're gonna see us.

BILLY I'm not waitin' anymore. It's makin' me crazy.

NATE You're not the only one.

BILLY No, I mean I don't have anythin' else. You've got your wife, your kids. Somethin' to go home to.

NATE Don't make me laugh. Not that I'm blamin' Rosie.

BILLY I got nothin'. Nobody.

NATE I thought you said you were seein' somebody.

BILLY Ya, but it's not somebody I should be seein'.

NATE What are you talkin' about?

BILLY You know the groceries? The ladies I been bringin' food too?

NATE Ya…

BILLY Well, one a' them was pretty lonely. Practically ripped my clothes off.

NATE You son of a…. You're doin' somebody's wife?

BILLY She said their marriage was already over.

NATE They always say that.

BILLY That's what happens if you leave home. When the cat's away…

NATE is taken aback. He considers for a moment.

NATE No. Rose would never do anythin' like that.

BILLY I didn't mean her.

NATE *(He considers again.)* No, she wouldn't.

BILLY Anyway, we gotta do somethin' to end this. I gotta get movin'. Get my job back.

NATE Ya...

BILLY Come on. Let's go.

NATE Okay!

They slip through the gate in the fence, and jump up to a higher level. The mill soundscape is heard. BILLY and NATE move along in the shadows, creeping higher, as they climb along. Then they start to climb down. When they jump down, they open the paper bag, and are crouched over it.

Three men enter in silhouette, and see BILLY and NATE. They call to them. BILLY jumps up the fence and climbs up to a higher level. NATE is surrounded. The men start to beat NATE, as BILLY watches. BILLY calls to NATE, but does not jump down to help him. The mill sounds rise to a roar. BILLY runs away, leaving NATE alone. NATE is thrown out of the gate by the men. He collapses, as ALICE, MARIE and LOUIS run on to help him. REG sees NATE and runs off. The soundscape is gone.

ALICE Get some water!

LOUIS He need a doctor!

MARIE Damn criminals!

She runs off to get water.

ALICE Nate. Nate, are you all right?

NATE Ya, ya, *(He tries to get up, but is in too much pain.)* Ummmph.

ALICE Stay there. Stay still.

NATE I just need a minute.

LOUIS What happen to Billy?

ALICE *(to NATE)* Wudna he with you?

NATE Maybe he's still in there.

MARIE returns with some rags and some water.

MARIE Here.

ALICE Now we'll get you all cleaned up, dearie. There you go.

ALICE starts to wipe the dirt and blood from NATE's head. He is sitting up.

LOUIS *(shaking his fist at the plant and the scabs)* We should go in there an' give 'em hell.

MARIE Oh ya, that would be great! Get everybody beat up.

LOUIS Well, I'm not gonna stand here. Do nothin'.

MARIE I don't want you to get hurt.

LOUIS Who's gonna hurt me?

MARIE I will, if you don't shut up!

LOUIS Look what they did!

MARIE I know, it's terrible, but we're not gonna fight.

LOUIS What you want me to do?

MARIE Stay here with me as long as it takes. Take care of me!

LOUIS I will!

MARIE & LOUIS Okay!

REG enters with ROSE. She stops when she sees NATE on the ground and covers her mouth in horror. NATE sees her, and stands with ALICE's help. ROSE runs to him. She embraces him. NATE winces a bit, but embraces her back. The others step away, giving them some room.

ROSE *(tenderly)* Are you all right?

NATE Ya.... How are you?

ROSE We're survivin'. You look awful.

NATE I guess I had it comin'.

ROSE Ya, you probably did.

NATE I miss you, Rosie.

ROSE Let's go home.

NATE I'm gonna change, you know.

ROSE No you won't. *(She takes him by the arm.)* How long you been wearing that shirt?

NATE Since I left.

ROSE Oh, Nate.

ROSE takes the cloth from his hand, and wipes his face. NATE closes his eyes and lets her. BILLY enters. The others look at him with anger.

BILLY Nate?

NATE turns and looks at BILLY.

NATE Where'd you go?

BILLY I thought you was behind me.

ALICE D' you see where your fightin' gets you?

LOUIS Nate coulda been killed.

BILLY He's pretty tough.

MARIE So are we all. But we're not fightin'.

ALICE It's not the way, Billy.

BILLY Maybe not your way.

REG You still think this is right? After all this? All of us fightin' each other? Nate gettin' beaten? And God knows what you were gonna do if you hadn't been seen. How many of the men inside would have been hurt? Does someone have to die? Is that when you'll stop?

BILLY I don't know.

ALICE Well, if you don't, someone's gonna get hurt, or killed, an' it might be one of us.

ROSE It might be you.

REG Unless you stop.

BILLY turns away from them.

BILLY Maybe that's what we need.

REG No, Billy! That's not what we need. They'll crack your head open and put you in jail. Then you'll have no job. Nothin'! Think about it. We're fightin' for the Union, for 1005, and if you get hurt, or arrested, you won't be comin' back to work when this is over.

BILLY It's never gonna be over!

REG Yes it is! We're gonna win, and when we do, you gotta be there to take your job back. That's what this is all about! Why we come here every day, and march round and round. Why we will not give in.

ALICE You have to think about why you're doin' this. An' take responsibility for your actions.

BILLY I do.

ROSE Even Myrtle Gibson?

Beat. BILLY says nothing. A low mechanical noise creeps in at a low volume.

ALICE What about Myrtle?

ROSE I heard that Billy's been bringin' her food.

ALICE Yes, while Frank's been inside. They've been havin' a hard time.

NATE Myrtle the one you've been spendin' time with?

BILLY She was lonely.

ALICE *(realizing what has been going on)* Oh, Billy.

MARIE Oh *Dio.*

ALICE I asked you to bring her groceries!

BILLY You asked me to help her.

The noise is getting louder now.

REG Myrtle is married to my brother.

BILLY I know! I didn't ask for it to happen.

REG You can't do that! You can't just go through life not thinking, or caring what's gonna happen to you, or to other people!

BILLY Like you do, Reg? Did you think what this strike was gonna do? About all the people that were gonna get hurt? How many were gonna be ruined? When you were yelling at us to vote for this strike? Do you think about that?

REG I… *(beat)* I do. I think about it all the time.

The noise is louder now. They begin to notice it.

LOUIS What's that?

MARIE What is that sound?

BILLY It's a train. I saw it when I was inside.

ALICE A train?

BILLY Loaded with steel.

NATE *(realizing)* They're comin' out!

LOUIS We gotta warn them. On the line!

REG They're tryin' to break through the line!

LOUIS *(shouting to attract strikers off stage)* TRAIN!

REG We gotta stop them.

LOUIS TRAIN!

NATE Get up to the gate!

ROSE We can't stop a train. Nate! Don't!

The stage darkens. The light from the train inside the plant pierces the darkness and moves forward. It looks like the train is coming through the lines. There is chaos on stage: screams, shouts, bangs, sounds of a train, smoke, and confusion. Silhouetted images of men fighting are caught in the beam of light. The train tries to advance through the gates, but is blocked by the strikers. A lone man (REG) stands in front of the train. Finally the train backs into the plant, and the gates are closed. The lights and the sounds fade.

As the smoke from the train clears, the crowd disperses. REG is down left, and sees a figure up on the scaffolding.

REG Frank? Is that you? Frank!

FRANK looks down at REG, then turns to move away from him and head back into the plant.

Wait, Frank.

REG climbs up the scaffolding, up to the second level.

Are you all right?

FRANK Ya. *(beat)* You?

REG Just a few scratches. Nothin' a few beers won't fix.

FRANK Someone coulda been killed.

REG Coulda. Ya.

Beat.

FRANK I talked with Myrtle this morning on the phone. Someone's broken a couple of our windows, and painted stuff on the house.

REG What did they paint on the house?

FRANK You know damn well. S.C.A.B. She's alone in there with the kids, and she's scared. I told her you would look after her.

REG What the hell can I do? It's happening all over town. I can't look after everybody. Why don't you come out here and look after your own family?

FRANK *(agitated)* You think this has been easy? Havin' my wife and kids terrified?

REG Then why are you in here?

FRANK 'Cause we're makin' steel. I work eight hours out of twenty four, and spend the rest of the time trapped in here, crazy with boredom, worryin' about my family.

REG I'm takin' a lot of flack out here too. Some of it because of you.

FRANK turns to leave.

No... wait.

Beat. The two brothers look at each other. Then REG turns and looks out, balancing on the edge, as they did when they were kids.

I need your help.

FRANK What?

REG How do I end this thing?

FRANK Why should I help you?

REG We take care of each other.

Beat. FRANK looks out over the city as well.

FRANK You don't need my help. You said it a minute ago. It's happening all over town. Think about it. The whole city is on your side. The people of this city support the union. They are the union. All you have to do is get them involved.

REG How?

FRANK How do I know? Bring 'em down here. Have a march or somethin'.

REG A march.... Like a parade? Maybe we could get people out for that.

The two brothers are balancing in the wind, on the second level of the scaffolding of the mill, like they did when they were boys.

FRANK Ya, that might do it.

FRANK turns to leave.

REG Frankie. *(FRANK stops.)* I'll get Alice to call Myrtle. They can stay at our place for a while.

FRANK Thanks.

REG Why don't you come out, Frank? If you come out now, the guys'll welcome you. If you wait, you're goin' to have to live with this thing forever.

FRANK I made my choice.

REG I don't understand why you're stayin' in!

FRANK I guess for the same reason you're stayin' out. I think I'm right.

FRANK turns and climbs down into the plant. REG stays up on the second level, thinking.

Cross fade to HILTON at his desk, his head in his hands. KELLY enters his office.

KELLY The train was a bust – forced back by the strikers. The fighting sent people to the hospital, and they're blaming us for it. Five hundred OPP and RCMP officers are pouring into the city. They're gearing up for a showdown. Strikers against the police.

HILTON That's exactly what we want, isn't it? They'll put an end to the strike.

KELLY The police might break the picket line, but they'll break the company in the process. All over the country, union leaders are talking about a general strike in solidarity with their brothers at Stelco. Well done, Mr. Hilton. *(sarcastic)* Your way seems to be working.

KELLY exits.

Cross fade to the strikers down on the line. NATE's arm is in a sling. BILLY is urging the group to action.

BILLY The cops are on their way, comin' to smash heads. Nate, we've got to set up barricades, be ready for them.

NATE I went in with you once. That was enough.

BILLY We've got to shut the plant down!

MARIE That's all we need, an all-out war.

ALICE We canna do a thing until we hear from the union leaders. Reg is down there with Millard and Sefton and all the top men.

BILLY It's been three months, Alice!

ALICE I know. And we'll hold out three more if we have to. *(beat)* You've done enough, don't you think? I know you've been hurt, but you don't need to be passin' it on. Eh comrade? *(gently)* Come now. *(She touches him and smiles.)* Enough.

BILLY hangs his head. REG rushes in.

REG Alice!

The others turn to him expectantly, hoping for good news.

ALICE What'd they say?

LOUIS What's gonna happen?

REG We're organizing a parade.

MARIE What?

NATE *(disdainful)* Come on, Reg.

REG No, it's gonna work. Listen. A big parade, the whole city marching in solidarity with the union men.

ALICE How do we know they'll join us?

REG The leaders have been canvassing all the groups. Church groups, service clubs. Everyone is with us!

BILLY What good will a parade do?

REG Billy, all the veterans are with us. The police won't fire on us if we're wearing our country's uniforms.

ROSE It might work.

ALICE This is the show of strength you wanted.

REG This is how we win this strike!

Music of a marching band comes in low.

MARIE What do we do?

REG Spread the word! Tell everyone you can think of that they gotta be in the parade.

ALICE The wives we've been givin' the groceries to.

MARIE The Italian Club.

ROSE The Ukrainians!

BILLY The Communists!

REG We're gonna need you with them, Billy, to keep them in line. We'll meet at the plant gates.

BILLY shakes REG's hand. Then he hugs him quickly, and runs off.

The music of the marching band increases in volume. The group moves down stage. LOUIS and NATE put on their army jackets.

ALICE We'll march through the city.

NATE Hundreds of vets'll join us.

LOUIS All in their uniforms, wearin' the medals they won.

MARIE We'll fill the streets.

NATE It'll be just like bein' back in the army again.

ROSE We'll feel the surge of power.

ALICE There's ten thousand of us at least.

LOUIS Cheerin' and yellin'.

REG All the way down to Woodlands Park.

The music continues and the cast continues to march. MARIE waves to onlookers lining the streets. LOUIS and ROSE join. There is a sense of joy and exuberance. Sounds of crowds cheering can be heard.

Cross fade to HILTON in his office. KELLY rushes in. The sounds of the march diminishes but can still be heard in the background.

KELLY Mr. Hilton! The whole city is marching!

HILTON Where are the police?

KELLY They're watching the parade!

HILTON Why don't they attack?

KELLY Soldiers are marching with the workers – veterans, decorated heroes. These men and women were fighting for their country less than a year ago. The police can't attack them!

HILTON They don't understand what they're doing.

KELLY I think they do. *(beat)* This city is standing up.

HILTON What do we do?

KELLY The Board of Directors wants you to settle.

HILTON SETTLE?

KELLY *(nodding)* With the union.

HILTON There is no union, damn it!

KELLY Then what is that?!

She gestures out to the crowds. Beat. HILTON rises and looks out at the marchers.

HILTON *(resigned)* Call Millard. Tell him if they can sign half of the men, they can – they can have their union.

The strikers erupt in cheers and everyone hugs each other. The marching music rises in volume, and the group begins to dance to it. KELLY and HILTON come down and watch the celebrations but HILTON hangs back.

The gates to the plant open, and FRANK emerges with his kit bag. REG and the others see FRANK coming out. Everyone stops dancing. FRANK is distraught. He looks at REG and then turns away from him. REG hangs his head. ALICE moves to hold his hand.

MARIE and LOUIS are holding on to each other, as are ROSE and NATE. A banner is unfurled reading: "Steelworker Local 1005."

BILLY comes to the front of the stage and the others flank him in the same arrangement that they were in at the opening to the play. Each individual is illuminated by spots.

BILLY Things changed that day. *(beat)* I met my wife, Evie, in that parade. *(beat)* I tore up my Communist Party card. *(beat)* We had three kids and eventually owned a big house, up in the south end of town. *(beat)* I changed. We all changed.

Beat.

Reg, he ended up in provincial politics. He was good at it too – with Alice's help.

Beat. The spots fade over REG and ALICE.

Marie and Louis had a bunch of kids. Louis wouldn't let any of them work at Stelco.

Beat. The spots fade over MARIE and LOUIS.

Nate worked in the bar mills for thirty more years, sweatin' and burnin' until the day he walked out of the mill for the last time.

Rose said their oldest, Bobby, ended up workin' at the Stelco head office in Toronto. Don't know which Nate thought was worse: that Bobby was in management, or that he lived in Toronto.

Beat. The spots fade over NATE and ROSE.

Frank stayed with Stelco until he retired. Never did join the union. A lot of strikers never spoke to a scab the rest of their days.

Beat. The spot fades over FRANK.

The '46 Stelco strike was a victory won on the picket line. It changed the way workers were treated in this country… how people treated each other.

The lights come up and the cast, including FRANK, KELLY and HILTON, join BILLY at centre stage. "Which Side Are You On?" is sung as a triumphal anthem.

BILLY Come all of you good workers,
Good news to you I'll tell
Of how that good old union
Has come in here to dwell.

MEN Which side are you on?
WOMEN Which side are you on?
BILLY Which side are you on?
MEN Which side are you on?
BILLY Which side are you on?
ALL Oh, which side are you on?

EVERYONE My daddy was a Steel Man
And I'm a Steel Man's son
And I'll stick with the union
'Til every battle's won

WOMEN Which side are you on?
MEN Oh, which side are you on?
EVERYONE Which side are you on?
Oh, which side are you on?

Come all of you good workers
Good news to you I'll tell
Of how that good old union
Has come in here to dwell.

All antiphonal unison and harmonies.

WOMEN Which side are you on?
MEN Which side are you on?
EVERYONE Which side are you on?
Oh which side are you on?
Which side are you on?
Oh which side are you on?

The cast bows and dances off the stage.

Historical Photo Gallery Sources

(from pages 35–40)

Page 35
top: Labour Studies, McMaster University LS430-H.
bottom: Labour Studies, McMaster University ls048-h.

Page 36
Hamilton Public Library

Page 37
top: Labour Studies, McMaster University ls246-h.
bottom: Labour Studies, McMaster University ls048-h.

Page 38
top: Labour Studies, McMaster University LS581-H.
bottom: Labour Studies, McMaster University

Page 39
top: Labour Studies, McMaster University
bottom: Labour Studies, McMaster University ls114-h.

Page 40
Labour Studies, McMaster University LS599-H.

Charles T. Cozens is an internationally known arranger, orchestrator, composer, conductor, music director and producer. Labelled by the Canadian press as "one of Canada's premiere arrangers," Mr. Cozens is a past winner of the CBC National Workshop Arranger's Competition.

Since then, his orchestral arrangements have been performed consistently by major orchestras in North America and Europe to critical acclaim.

Writing credits include the Canadian Brass, Hannaford Street Silver Band, Quartetto Gelato, the Nylons, several theatrical musicals including *Swingstep* (Dora Award) and more than 50 CD recordings for Somerset/ Universal, Solitudes, Avalon, Reflections, Capitol, Attic, CBC SM 5000, BMG International, Victor and Jazz Inspiration.

His conducting credits include most major Symphony Orchestras in Canada, more than 40 musicals including *Beauty And The Beast, Man of LaMancha* and *Cats* and a plethora of CD recordings and film and television soundtracks.

Recent writing and conducting credits include two new symphonic recordings with the Moscow Radio Symphony Orchestra and The Russian National Symphony Orchestra at MosFilm studios in Moscow.

In 2003, Mr. Cozens was presented with the Established Performing Artist Award from the Mississauga Arts Council and in 2006, was nominated for a Juno Award for his album "Balance" (Instrumental Album Of The Year).

For more information, please visit www.charlescozens.com.

photo by David Laurence Photo

Bill Freeman is an award-winning author who has written historical fiction for young adults, film scripts, documentaries, theatrical plays, educational videos and non-fiction books. He specializes in writing about Canada and the Canadian experience.

In the 1960s and 70s Bill lived, worked and studied in Hamilton. The play *Glory Days*, is part of his exploration of the life of the city and its fascinating history.

Bill is perhaps best known as the author of novels for young adults set in Canada in the latter part of the nineteenth century called the Bains Series. He is also well known for his books of popular history. His most recent work, *Hamilton: A People's History*, surveys the city's often turbulent history. Many of his books have received high critical acclaim and a number of awards.

In recent years Bill has worked in the film industry as a writer and historical consultant. He has been on the creative team of many film projects as writer, narrator and consultant. The projects include a science series for high school students and "Mighty Machines II," a made for television project for pre-school children.

Bill Freeman lives on Toronto Island with his partner Paulette.